DEHYDRATION
MADE SIMPLE

DEHYDRATION
MADE SIMPLE

MARY BELL

Magic Mill
Division of SSI
Salt Lake City, Utah

CONTENTS

FOREWORD

Like a culinary masterpiece which requires the skillful blending of choice ingredients, Mary Bell has the combination of special talents and interests which make her the ideal person to author a book on dehydration. As an enthusiastic backpacker, canoeist, and hiker, she long ago recognized the need for lightweight and portable foods. A dedication to physical fitness taught her the value of good nutrition and the importance of avoiding unwanted and unnecessary additives and chemicals. Her love of gardening and a desire to preserve the surplus of her labors created an interest in food preservation. And as a wife and mother she was interested in new ways to stretch the family food budget while adding variety to everyday meal planning. The ingredients led to a discovery of dehydration and a fascination with this convenient, nutritious, simple, and economical method of food preservation.

Mary has dehydrated an enormous variety of foods —from rose hips to tofu (soybean curd)—and developed and tested hundreds of recipes using dried foods. She has lectured extensively on the multiple benefits of dehydration and conducted numerous demonstrations. She was introduced to Magic Mill while conducting a marketing study of dehydrator manufacturers. Mary was as immediately taken with the Magic Aire II, its design, simplicity of operation, and results, as we were with her and her expertise. The mutually compatible relationship led to the publication of *Dehydration Made Simple*.

Just as this book represents many, many years of dehydration experience, so does the product which it endorses. Hundreds of dealers and distributors have tested commercial dehydrators. Magic Mill has developed several models. Refinement has been a long and tedious process. Input from our sales force has been invaluable. At last we are proud to present a product which lives up to the Magic Mill reputation for quality and dependability—the Magic Aire II.

You are about to find that dehydration has never been easier or more successful. We are pleased to introduce Mary Bell and her comprehensive dehydration guide, *Dehydration Made Simple*.

MAGIC MILL

PREFACE

Dehydration Made Simple began over a decade ago with one prolific zucchini plant. As an avid gardener I was looking for an easy and economical method of preserving surplus crops. I tried canning and freezing and found them to be tedious and time-consuming. Then I discovered dehydration. My love of the outdoors had already introduced me to the convenience of commercially dried products, but suddenly I found just how easily I could prepare my own dehydrated foods.

I experimented with sun drying and oven drying with minimal success before purchasing my first electric dehydrator. It enabled me to dry meats, fish, vegetables, and herbs, in addition to fruits. My enthusiasm for dehydration grew. I set out to obtain the best electric food drier; I studied and tried several commercially available models. Then I came across the Magic Aire II.

The Magic Aire II is unquestionably the most sophisticated, reliable, and efficient dehydrator I have used. It's attractive; it's easy to clean; and best of all, it makes dehydration simple. I found that there is no need to pretreat foods with the Magic Aire II. It dries most foods beautifully without blanching or dipping, although I included pretreatment procedures as an option in this book.

Other features of the Magic Aire II which I love include the stackable trays which enable you to use as few as two or as many as ten trays. The preset temperature makes the process totally reliable and fail-safe. The air flow system is masterfully designed and engineered. And the Magic Aire II accessories —the Fruit Leather Sheets and Garden Magic Sprouting Trays—make it possible to dry fruit and vegetable leathers and finely chopped or grated foods.

As dehydrated foods became more and more a part of our family diet, my recipe collection grew. My desire to share these ideas, along with the need I recognized for more complete dehydration information, led me to write *Dehydration Made Simple*. Included are some of my favorite recipes. Try the Granola with Dried Fruit (page 63) for breakfast. The French Onion Soup (page 41) rivals the Parisian's finest. You'll rave over the Apple Brownies (page 66). And for a deliciously different snack, try dipping dried zucchini chips in the Garlic-Curry Dip (page 110). Don't be afraid to experiment. This book reflects what I have found about home food dehydration. Use it as a guide, not as the last word. Alter my recipes to suit your preference. And use dehydrated foods in your own recipes.

As I developed these recipes I tried to be particularly nutrition conscious by minimizing the amounts of sugar, salt, and oil. Feel free to substitute whole wheat flour in any recipe, or use half whole wheat and half white. Honey or maple syrup may be used instead of sugar.

This book would not have been possible without the support and assistance of some very special people. Thank yous are extended to my husband Michael and my children, Sally and Eric, for their encouragement and for being my "guinea pigs." Thanks too to my parents, Harold and Helen Bell. I am appreciative of my friends and neighbors in the community who listened and talked to me about dehydration. Their suggestions, feedback, successful recipes, unsuccessful recipes, questions I could answer, and questions I could not all helped me to compile this book.

I am indebted to Robert Pedersen, Jim Harrison, and Bob Warden of Magic Mill for their belief in me and in this book. A generous thanks goes to Linda Prusse for her proficient editing, to Diane Browning for so beautifully composing the photographs, to Longin Lonczyna for his photographic skill, and to Steve Larsen for his excellent graphic design. This book is more than a recipe and instruction book; it is the reflection of many efforts from many sharing people.

Have fun with dehydration and *Dehydration Made Simple!*

INTRODUCTION

Welcome to the world of dehydration. You are about to rediscover the oldest known form of food preservation. Dehydration and drying are interchangeable terms. Both refer to the method of preserving food by eliminating the moisture. When moisture is returned to dried foods, the terms rehydration and reconstitution are used. *Dehydration Made Simple* will do just as the title implies—make this oldest form of food preservation a simple, new, and delightful way to preserve food and thus provide added nutrition and budget savings.

History of Dried Foods

Food drying was discovered out of necessity because fresh food was not always available. By exposing seasonal foods to the natural drying powers of the sun and the wind and thereby removing the moisture, fruits, vegetables, grains, legumes, and meats could be kept almost indefinitely. Nature—the sun and the wind—was the exclusive tool for preserving perishable foods. Yet success depended on luck and ingenuity, as the sun and the wind were unpredictable and slow. Food that was left to dry in the open fields often fell prey to the elements and to wild animals, birds, and insects. Often only a small portion was finally preserved.

The practice of food drying has continued for centuries, spreading from one continent to another. Without dried foods the nomadic lifestyle would have been impossible, for nomads could only remain transient if they had a continual supply of food. Dehydration was one way to assure an adequate supply. By preserving the surplus of the harvest, people the world over learned that they could endure times of uncertainty, drought, and famine.

Different cultures perfected the art of drying foods indigenous to their particular environments. The Greeks and Romans dried peas and grapes; the Persians preserved dates, apricots, and melons; and the Chinese and Japanese cured fish, eggs, and rice. Mongolian explorers packed bundles of dried milk to sustain themselves on their long journeys. American settlers, observing the practice of sun drying food among the North American Indians, learned to preserve corn, squash, buffalo, and venison as they pioneered westward. Thus, for thousands of years the custom of drying perishable foods has endured, and the tradition of dehydration has been retained.

The industrial revolution of the 1900s accounted for the decline in food drying and was responsible for the easy accessibility of canned foods. In recent times, the techniques of commercial dehydration and freeze-drying advanced, while home drying was replaced, in part, by home and commercial canning.

The launching of the space program brought with it the necessity of producing food that was both nutritious and compact for use by astronauts in outerspace. The twentieth century transformed the art of food drying into a science—the science of dehydration. The success of food preservation is no longer dependent on luck and happenstance, for advanced technology has been applied to the basic principles of dehydration: constant controlled heat and circulating air.

Today, the electric food dryer has made it possible for people to again dry food at home and enjoy dehydrated foods with greater convenience and significant economic savings. Dried foods are popular with homemakers as well as with outdoor enthusiasts, such as canoeists, bicyclists, skiers, hunters, and backpackers. More and more budget-conscious families are rediscovering food dehydration as a practical solution to meal planning and preparation.

Whether an ancient art or a modern science, the tradition of dehydration is available to you and your family. You can dry fresh fruits and vegetables gathered from the garden; seasonal crops harvested at their nutritional peak; trimmings, such as peels, seeds, and leaves, often discarded as waste; leftovers frequently forgotten in the refrigerator; and bargain foods purchased from the grocery store or the farmers' market. The art of dehydrating foods leads to a marvelous awareness of the rich, sweet, natural taste, and the nutritional value of foods.

Why Dehydration

Dehydration is becoming a popular and preferred method of preserving and storing food. The drying process retards bacterial growth, the common cause of food decomposition and spoilage. Without water, food cannot spoil; it is preserved for future use.

Generally speaking, fresh food is considered the best source of nutrition. But unfortunately, seasonal changes limit the time in which to grow and enjoy fresh foods. Since few can grow fresh fruits and vegetables year round, foods are purchased at inflated prices through the local grocery store, where the quality of produce is substantially different. Nika Hazelton in *The Unabridged Vegetable Cookbook* makes this comparison:

> *The supermarket green bean must have a high fiber content so that it can remain on the shelves for a week before wilting, whereas the home gardener's tender, low-fiber bean goes into the pot soon after it is picked.*

> *The commercial producer needs tomatoes that do not crack, that stand up to mechanical harvesting,*

Dried foods for the great outdoors (from left to right, top to bottom): vegetable soup mix, peaches, apples, fruit leather, fish and beef jerky, Granola with Dried Fruit (page 63), and Gorp (page 61)

that come off the plant easily, that mature uniformly, and that ship well. Some growers say that to transport a fully ripened tomato would be either impossible or prohibitively expensive. Consequently, commercially grown tomatoes have to be harvested when immature and then allowed to ripen in transit and after reaching their destination. Locally grown tomatoes can be ripened fully on the vine, and there is no need for me to go into the flavor differences. The reason many supermarkets, even at the height of the local tomato season, sell their anemic-looking imitations of the real thing is that many supermarkets find it simpler to order from growers thousands of miles away because local tomatoes are too tender (is this an euphemism for being ripe, I wonder?) and therefore bruisable and wasteful in the distribution to the supermarket chain's branch stores.

(From the *Unabridged Vegetable Cookbook*, copyright © 1976, by Nika Hazelton. Reproduced by permission of publisher, M. Evans and Company, Inc., New York, New York 10017.)

With an electric food dryer you can enjoy vine-ripened flavor and substantial savings. Fruits and vegetables can be bought in season at low prices. Bargain foods can be purchased from the grocery store in large quantities when the cost is low. The harvest of summer gardens and produce from farmers' roadside stands offer foods rich in nutrition at reasonable costs. Buy fruits, vegetables, meats, and herbs on sale. Use what you want fresh and then dehydrate the remainder to enjoy long after the season and the sales are over. Herbs gathered and dried in summer are delicious substitutes for the expensive bottled ones. Dehydrating fresh foods for use later in the year helps you to avoid the high cost of buying supermarket produce during the "off season."

Many people today know the value of having a food storage supply. Food stored away for use during lean times gives a sense of security against shortages, strikes, and economic uncertainty. Dehydrated food can be safety stored. For storing dehydrated foods you will need glass jars (recycled ones work just fine), coffee or shortening cans with lids, canisters, or sealable airtight plastic bags. Because they have been condensed both in size and in weight, dried foods can be stored in one-third, one-tenth, or even less space than needed for fresh, canned, or frozen foods.

DEHYDRATION VERSUS HOME CANNING

Compared with home canning, dehydration involves less work. To dehydrate food, you simply cut the food, place it on the drying trays of the home dehydrator, remove the food when it is dry, and store it. Canning requires cutting, peeling, packing in jars, preparing sugar syrups, sealing bottles, hot water processing or pressure canning, and storing. The process is cumbersome and time-consuming.

Home dehydration is also less expensive than canning. The electric dehydrator costs only pennies a day to operate and requires a one-time cost. No need to continually buy canning jars or canning equipment; any container with a tight lid works well for storage of dried foods.

Consider these other advantages: In canning, jars have to be filled and sealed, and they cannot be opened until they are to be used. With dehydration, jars can be filled and ingredients used or added at your convenience. Peelings, seeds, leaves, leftovers, and cooked vegetables which are usually discarded can be dried and saved for use in soups, hot dishes, and salads. Think of the savings to the budget. In dehydration any amount can be dried at your convenience. A variety of foods can be processed immediately after harvesting. You can dry anything from a bushel of apples to the leftover leaves of celery stalks to the lima beans from last night's dinner.

In canning, you add water to the food, thus increasing the bulk and diluting the food value. In dehydration the process is reversed; you remove water, dramatically decreasing the quantity but not the quality of the food. There's no need to reserve a lot of shelf, closet, or storage space for your dried foods.

DEHYDRATION VERSUS FREEZING

Freezing has many of the same disadvantages as canning. Frozen foods are bulky. The freezer must be operated constantly, making it very costly to keep the water in the food frozen over a period of time, thus the food in your freezer becomes expensive even if purchased on sale.

Dried foods are safer and more nutritious than frozen foods, as foods kept in the freezer are susceptible to spoilage if there is a power outage or machine breakdown. When frozen foods are blanched before freezing (and this happens frequently), valuable nutrients are lost long before you're ready to serve a meal. Plus when you take frozen foods out of the freezer, you must use the whole amount; whereas with dried food you take only what you need.

Advantages of Dehydration

VERSATILITY

Lightweight, dried foods can be used in a variety of ways: They make tasty, nutritional snacks and great additions to brown-bag lunches; they become convenient meals for travelers; and because they are a source of quick energy and are compact in size and volume, they are ideal to take along while enjoying outdoor sports.

Dried foods combine easily in favorite recipes. They can be used to make delicious beverages, added to desserts, or served as main courses. Dehydrated foods make wonderful additions to jams, jellies, granolas, jerkys, leathers, hot dishes, and teas. New foods, such as fruit leather (dried pureed fruit batter and flavorings) and meat jerky (dried meat and flavorings), are concentrated foods rich in nutritional values.

TASTE

Many dried foods, especially those used in cooking, are indistinguishable from fresh foods; cooked, dried spinach, dried eggplant used in recipes, and dried fruit in baking are a few examples.

The taste of certain foods is intensified by the dehydration process, especially some vegetables. Fruits are sweeter because the removal of water concentrates the fruit sugars. Dried herbs are two to three times stronger and more flavorful than fresh herbs.

Some foods will taste quite different when dried, as drying changes these foods in a manner similar to foods that have been canned, frozen, or placed in cold storage. Cucumbers, tomatoes, pumpkin, and jerky (to name a few) do not return to their original texture or flavor, but they can still be used in creative, new ways. Check under each individual food for ideas and recipe suggestions.

Foods that are overripe may have a slightly fermented taste and a poor texture after they are dried. Foods that are underripe, bruised or damaged may have less flavor than riper food, and this will be reflected in the dried product. Home dehydrated foods may taste different from commercially produced foods because of the various pretreatments and the methods of preparation and packaging.

When water or liquid is restored to dehydrated foods the taste is exciting, new, and wholesome. The flavor can be compared to the taste of garden-fresh fruits and vegetables. Dried foods have a natural taste that the average grocery store customer rarely has a chance to experience. Using dehydrated fruits, vegetables, and meats gives you an opportunity to enjoy a unique taste experience as well as a significant monetary savings.

NUTRITION

With the alternative of dehydration, you can control the quality of your food; food can be preserved at its nutritional height. Dehydration captures the full value and rich taste of foods. And here's a real plus, dehydration does not require the use of additives, chemicals, or any other food preservatives. Foods do not need to be pretreated before drying, so you avoid nutrient loss and the addition of chemicals.

Drying food is a natural way to capture and condense food value—only the water is removed. According to a nutrition study, "The effect of water removal on nutritional changes of dehydrated foods is relatively small if the dehydration temperature is kept moderate and the food is adequately packaged." (From the *Nutritional Evaluation of Food Processing*, copyright © 1975, by Endel Karmas. Used by permission of publisher, A.V.I. Publishing Company, West Port, Connecticut 06880.) Most foods contain large quantities of water, and when this is removed the sugar is concentrated. Everything that contains natural sugar becomes sweeter when dehydrated. Dehydrated treats are a healthy, natural alternative to using processed sugar and storebought snacks.

Through the dry-heat process used in dehydration, natural vitamins and minerals are retained. Research available on the nutritional evaluations of home food drying is, at this point, inadequate. Most studies and nutritional evaluations are made using commercially dehydrated foods. Many home-drying enthusiasts believe that home food drying provides a product that is far superior to any commercial product because vitamins are retained through the quick processing without using chemicals.

Because food dehydration offers a lower exposure to high temperatures than canning and therefore destroys fewer vitamins, it is an excellent method of food preservation. The loss of nutritive value during drying is very small in comparison to losses which occur during cooking and canning.

The fiber and energy content of dehydrated foods is the same as or more than that found in fresh foods. The peels and skins of fruits and vegetables contain many vitamins and minerals and need not be removed from the food for drying.

Dryers Versus Other Dehydration Methods

Dehydrating can be done by a number of methods; sun drying and oven drying are the most common, but several other methods have been used to some extent. The controlled environment provided by an electric dehydrator is by far the most successful.

Sun drying has several disadvantages. First, only a few foods can be sun dried successfully and safely. Foods having a low sugar and acid content, such as meats, fish, and vegetables, can spoil during the sun-drying process because it takes 4 to 6 days. Second, sun drying tends to lower the quality and nutritional value of foods as compared to those dried under the controlled conditions obtained with a dehydrator. Third, when drying foods in the sun, it is nearly impossible to attain sanitary conditions. Fourth, with sun drying you are entirely at the mercy of the weather. A sudden rain can cause the loss of hours of labor, in addition to the cost of the food you are drying. Fifth, vegetables must be dried to a 5 percent or lower moisture content in order to store well. This is almost impossible with sun drying because exposure to sunlight for more than a day or so can produce sunburn and scorching before reaching the 5 percent moisture levels. Sixth, sun drying is not recommended for herbs and spices because they lose their aroma, flavor, oil, and color.

Oven drying also has several serious disadvantages, the biggest being the cost of the gas or electricity used. Drying in an oven takes two to three times longer than drying in a dehydrator, and it uses far more energy each hour. A second problem is poor temperature control. Most ovens are too hot, and it is difficult to maintain a constant temperature. In many cases the food is cooked before it is dry. Third, it is extremely difficult to oven dry foods containing a high moisture content, such as tomatoes, as their skins prevent evaporation. Fourth, food dried in an oven is darker, more brittle, and less flavorful than foods dried in a dehydrator. Fifth, there is no air circulation which is essential in good food drying.

Other methods for dehydrating foods include solar drying, room drying, and stove-top drying. All are inefficient and present even more problems than sun drying or oven drying.

Dehydrators are the answer. It is an accepted fact that a good-quality, factory-made dehydrator will yield a better-quality dried product than will any other method of drying. A high-quality dehydrator eliminates all the problems associated with other methods of dehydration; it provides the controlled environment needed for efficient and nutritional drying of foods; it allows you to dry foods 24 hours a day without worrying about weather; it elimi- nates unsanitary conditions; it dries food in a mini- mum amount of time; it dries fruits, vegetables, and meats beautifully; and it is economical to operate (only a few cents to dehydrate a large quan- tity of food). As more and more people become interested in dehydration, several dehydrators have been put on the market, and as in all products, the quality of the units varies. Throughout this book reference has been made to the Magic Aire II Food Dehydrator for it is the opinion of the author that it is the best.

What to Dehydrate

You can dehydrate almost anything—vegetables, fruits, meats, fish, poultry, herbs, and flowers. You will be amazed at the variety. Try everything, ex- periment with new foods in old recipes—see what you like and don't like.

Overripe, canned, or small amounts of leftover fruits make terrific fruit leathers. Leftover vegetables can be pureed and dried as leathers then powdered and used in soups, sauces, and breads.

Most dried foods, when cooked and served, are just as flavorful, if not more so, than fresh food. Some- times, but not always, it is hard to tell the differ- ence. But you don't have to cook all dried food. Dried fruits, thinly sliced vegetables, or beef jerky make tasty snacks without cooking.

Some dehydrators can also be used for drying dough crafts, seed nut plaques, and other craft projects if the goal is to remove water from the object.

Preparation

EQUIPMENT NEEDED

You do not need a great deal of special equipment for drying. In fact, you probably already have all the most necessary equipment in your kitchen. Here's a checklist:

- A sharp paring knife. Use stainless steel blades because carbon blades turn some fruits and vegetables dark. A vegetable slicer makes the job quicker. The Bosch Electronic Slicer is a great asset in the kitchen.
- A peeler.
- A cutting board.
- A blender for making leathers, flakes and powders. The Bosch Kitchen Machine is ideal for pureeing produce.
- A steamer and basket or a kettle and collap- sible steamer, if pretreating foods.
- Plastic wrap or the Magic Aire II Fruit Leather Sheets.
- Nylon netting, cheesecloth, or the Garden Magic Sprouting Trays.

DECIDE, THEN TRY

Before you begin drying foods, decide how they will be used. This will help you determine how thick to slice for drying, whether to peel or not, and whether to salt or season. Making plans before you begin eliminates the need to adjust recipes at cooking time.

If your family carries lunches to school or work, you may want an abundance of dried fruits that can be eaten "as is." If you do lots of baking, prepare now for peach pies and banana bread to be enjoyed in the months ahead. Dry shredded vegetables for use in cookies, pancakes, or quick breads. Lightly salt thinly sliced vegetables before drying to serve with yogurt or dips.

TO PEEL OR NOT TO PEEL

In general, if you peel fresh produce for a specific recipe, plan to peel the fruits or vegetables you intend to dehydrate. The peels of fruits and vegetables often contain much of the food's value and therefore should not be discarded. The peels of oranges, lemons, limes, tangerines, and other foods can be dried and then pulverized into a powder and added to many recipes.

For foods that will be eaten as snacks or used in dessert recipes, decide whether you want the peelings left on or removed. The peels of some foods, such as cucumbers, taste bitter in comparison to the sweetness of the pulp. This is especially true in foods having a high concentration of sugar. When fruits dry they sweeten, but the peels do not; therefore, the contrasting taste between the pulp and the peel is sometimes quite sharp.

CUTTING MAKES A DIFFERENCE

Moisture can escape during dehydration only from a cut or broken surface area in most food, not through its tough skin. Therefore, the larger the cut surface, the faster the food dehydrates. For this reason, thin stalks such as green beans, asparagus, and rhubarb are cut in half the long way or on an extreme diagonal (see illustration). Broccoli stems, depending on their diameter, should be halved or quartered. Small berries, such as cranberries, blueberries, strawberries, grapes, and cherries, should either be cut in half or blanched slightly to pop the skins.

Although wedges will dry in the dehydrator, the thin edge might be somewhat crisp before the thicker part is dry enough to store. Slicing the fruit across the core in the opposite direction (see illustration) will promote even, fast drying. Uniform pieces are easier to dry and to reconstitute. The smaller the pieces, the faster the drying.

Pretreatment

DIPPING

Some foods darken during the drying process. If you find this color change objectionable, food pieces may be dipped in solutions of lemon juice, orange juice, pineapple juice, ascorbic acid, or sodium bisulfite prior to dehydrating.

The most natural dipping solutions are fresh or bottled lemon, orange, or pineapple juice. Use full strength or prepare with 2 parts juice to 1 part water. Crystalline ascorbic acid may be obtained from drug stores or in stores selling canning and freezing supplies. Mix 1 teaspoon ascorbic acid per quart of water. When using sodium bisulfite, use 2 teaspoons per gallon of water. Dip fruit pieces or allow to soak up to 5 minutes. Drain the food pieces on paper towels before placing them on the dehydrator trays.

Dipping foods in pretreatment solutions is for appearance only, especially for fruits that oxidize easily; it is not necessary for the successful dehydration of food.

7

BLANCHING

Treating foods with boiling water or steam is called blanching. Blanching is a controversial issue in the dehydration process. One school of thought claims that blanching destroys some of the nutritional value of food because nutrients are dissolved in the boiling water and that the entire process is time-consuming and unnecessary. The other school of thought supports the idea that blanching sets the color of the food, stops enzyme action, promotes the long storage life of dried foods, induces faster dehydration because it softens the tissue of food, checks the ripening process, requires less soaking time before being used in cooking, and enhances the flavor and color of the rehydrated food when it is served. The choice is left to you. The Magic Aire II dries foods without pretreatment blanching.

There are two types of blanching: water-boil blanching and steam blanching. The choice of whether to steam blanch or water-boil blanch can best be made after experimenting with various foods and different types of preparation.

To water-boil blanch, bring 1 gallon of water to a boil in a large pot. Place 1 pound or 4 cups of food in a rack, strainer, or cheesecloth which will contain the food. Lower the container or place the food directly into the boiling water. The pan does not need to be covered. You can process as much food as can be covered by the constantly boiling water. Most foods are blanched in 3 to 6 minutes. Water-boil blanching requires two-thirds the time of steam blanching.

To steam blanch, bring about ½ gallon of water to a boil in a large pot. With a rack, colander, strainer, or cheesecloth, suspend the loosely arranged food pieces 2 inches above the boiling water. Replace the lid in order to contain the steam. You can process only one layer of food at a time with this process. Most foods are blanched in 4 to 8 minutes.

Using paper towels, drain blanched foods and then place on drying trays. Blanched foods need not be chilled before you place them on the dehydrator trays.

SULFURING

The sulfuring of food is not recommended when using an indoor food dehydrator because the sulfur fumes released in the air from the sulfured food may be dangerous to your health. Sulfured foods should be dried outdoors.

Sulfuring is done because it helps to prevent foods from darkening, to decrease drying time, and to preserve certain vitamins. In order to sulfur foods you need to construct a sulfur box. There are several books, including *How to Dry Foods, The Complete Book of Home Storage of Vegetables and Fruits,* and *Putting Food By* (see page 57), that give detailed direction on how to construct a sulfur box and how to safely sulfur food.

Filling the Trays

Once the food has been properly sliced and prepared, you are ready to fill the food dehydrator trays. Arrange the food pieces on the trays in a single layer with edges just touching. Do not overlap food. Some tray perforations should be uncovered to allow air to circulate; slices can be moved apart slightly to accomplish this. Place the pieces of food cut-side up on the tray.

During dehydration, shrinkage may cause smaller foods (peas, grated carrots, or chives) to fall through the tray perforations. To prevent this and other problems, as with herbs which may flake during dehydration, line the tray with nylon netting, needlepoint fabric, canvas, cheesecloth, or a similar coarsely woven fabric. Fabrics should be laundered before using. Cut a hole in the fabric for the center air-circulation hole.

Two accessories to the Magic Aire II can be a real boon to drying small or grated pieces of food. The finer screen of the Garden Magic Sprouter Trays makes them very useful for small pieces of food. The Magic Aire II Fruit Leather Sheets are thin plastic inserts especially made for drying leathers. They can be successfully used, however, for finely chopped foods. When using the fruit leather sheets, place one sheet on each dehydrator tray, alternating sides.

To dry chopped or shredded foods, spread the prepared food on a tray lined with nylon netting, the sprouter trays, or leather sheets. Food should not be thicker than ⅜ inch. Use a fork to separate the food in several spots to allow for circulation. It may be necessary to stir the foods once or twice during dehydration. When drying whole, round fruits, such as blueberries, fill the trays nearly to capacity and shake the trays to rotate the food surface.

To get the best possible dehydrating results from an electric food dehydrator, rotate the dehydrator shelves or trays from top to bottom at least once every 4 hours. By conscientiously rotating your shelves you will achieve more uniform drying.

Drying Time

It is difficult to state drying times because of variances in the amount of water in food, the cut and prepared size, and the humidity in the air. The soil conditions where the food was grown and the particular variety of food may also affect drying. The denser the food, the longer the drying time. The more surface area of the food exposed, the quicker the drying time. Experience will enable you to tell when you slice the food how long it takes to dry. Tomatoes, which are normally quite juicy, will take longer to dry than cabbage, which is more solid. Citrus fruits will take longer than apples.

Use the maps on pages 12 and 13 to determine the humidity level in your area. To use the map, locate where you live, check the color for your humidity level, and compare other areas in different months. The maps are color-coded to give the percentage of humidity in the outside air.

Check sliced vegetables, fruits, meats, and leathers periodically after about 4 hours of drying time. Check herbs and greens in 1 to 1½ hours, and chopped and shredded foods in 2 to 3 hours. Most vegetables take 2 to 10 hours to dry; most fruits 4 to 14 hours; meats, generally, 6 to 12 hours; herbs, greens and flowers, 2 hours. Vegetables are characteristically hard, crisp, leathery, or brittle when dry. Fruits are characteristically leathery, chewy, pliable, and elastic, and when cut with a knife there are no pockets of moisture. Meats, herbs, and flowers are hard when dry.

For long-term storage, dry foods until they are hard. For short-term storage, foods can be left softer, but check weekly for moisture collecting on the dried food, or when storing the dried foods in the refrigerator.

If foods have been dehydrated too long and become overdried or seem burnt, brittle, or slightly browned, they are still usable for soup or in most baked goods. They may take slightly longer to reconstitute and require additional water, but the flavor generally is not impaired.

If you wish to connect the dehydrator to an automatic timer, similar to those for turning lights off and on at a specific hour, be certain the timer has a capacity of at least 5 amps.

Storage

Once the food is sufficiently dehydrated to store, allow it to cool thoroughly—usually 15 to 30 minutes. If food is allowed to sit in the open air, it will begin to absorb moisture from the air. To lock in nature's goodness for a long and safe shelf life, select appropriate containers and a good storage location, as suggested below. For maximum preservation, store dried foods below 60° F. At temperatures of 80° F. food will begin to deteriorate in several months.

CONTAINERS

Any container that is clean, airtight, and moisture proof is suitable. There is no need to purchase special jars; recycle old ones. Glass jars with tight-fitting lids allow you to see the food. Dark glass jars are the best containers for storing dried foods, especially herbs, because the light will not be able to fade the dried food or to affect the nutrient and quality of the product. Heavy zippered plastic bags or heat-sealing cooking bags are also good. Use small bags, filling each one as full of food as possible to eliminate air. If you wish, these may then be placed in metal cans with lids to keep out insects. Shortening or coffee cans are good. A resealable plastic bagger works well because you can control bag size. Remove as much air from the bag as possible. Plastic containers with lids are fine, but because they are not often airtight, you should pack dried foods in plastic bags first. Seal and label the containers with the food name and date.

Do not use paper or cloth bags, lightweight plastic bags, bread wrappers, or any containers without a tight-fitting lid.

LOCATION

Remember "cool, dark, dry," for these are the keys to maintaining flavor, color, texture, and aroma. A pantry or closet is an ideal storage spot. Shelves near a window may need to be covered to keep out light. Clear glass jars or plastic containers should be placed in a dark paper bag or in a closed cabinet.

Dehydrated foods may be stored in the refrigerator, the freezer, or in the kitchen cupboard. Dried herbs can be stored in a glass jar (again, brown glass is best) and placed in the cupboard. Refrigerating dried meat is the safest way to insure continued freshness. Dried fruits and vegetables can be stored in airtight containers and placed almost anywhere.

Dried food will absorb both moisture and odor. And, as cement walls and floors are often damp, containers of dried foods should not be placed directly on the floor or touching a basement or cellar wall. To avoid absorption of odors, do not store dried foods near strong-smelling products, such as varnish, paint remover or kerosene.

9

LENGTH OF STORAGE

Dried foods store well. The following suggestions on length of storage will help you make maximum use of foods. Label and date dried foods; then use on a first-dried, first-to-use basis. Fruits and vegetables are best if not stored longer than one year. Continue to rotate regularly, using the first-dried, first-to-use rule in order to maintain a highly nutritious food storage plan. Leathers can be stored 6 months on the kitchen shelf, or longer if kept in the refrigerator, but meats and jerky may quickly develop a rancid taste if not kept refrigerated. Plan to use all meats, fish, poultry or jerky within a month or two. Herbs and flowers can be kept for years.

Check dried foods often for signs of mold, insects, or excessive moisture. If foods become more moist than when packed away, moisture is getting into the container through a leak or a loose-fitting lid. The food need not be discarded. It can again be spread on the dehydrator trays, redried, and packed back into airtight containers. Mold indicates that the foods were not dried sufficiently the first time. Discard moldy pieces and spread remainder on the dehydrator trays and redry.

To prolong the storage life of most dried foods even further, wrap in plastic wrap and store in freezer.

Rehydration

Rehydration is the process of restoring liquid to dried foods. This reconstitution is an important facet in learning how to use dehydrated foods. Water is removed from food in order to preserve it for future use. Some foods, especially vegetables, need to be soaked in or added to liquids to restore their moisture content before they can be consumed. All dehydrated foods, however, need not be rehydrated; fruits, fruit leathers, jerky, herbs, and flowers do not require rehydration. Dried fruits can be eaten as snacks, added to dessert recipes, or used in breakfast foods without rehydrating. Jerky can be eaten for a high-protein food. Herbs and flowers are added to other foods without rehydrating. Dry vegetables can be eaten as chips with dip, or added to soups or stews.

Often you will want to reconstitute dried foods before adding to recipes, using as side dishes, or combining with other ingredients. Try not to use more liquid than is necessary for rehydration because nutrients will be drained away along with the excess liquid. As a general rule, soak 1 cup dried food in 1 cup liquid and gradually add more liquid until the desired texture is obtained and the food will not absorb any more liquid. If you must drain reconstituted foods, save the liquid and try to find

a use for it; use as a fruit or vegetable juice; substitute the rehydration liquid for a different liquid called for in recipes; add to soups or stews; save to use for rehydrating other foods; freeze for use in soups, leathers, pies or compotes. Rehydration liquid has great nutritional value—don't pour it down the drain.

Vegetables can be soaked in water, soup broth, or vegetable juices and will usually rehydrate within 1 to 2 hours. But depending on the size of the dried food pieces and the degree to which the pieces have been dried, rehydration may take as long as 8 hours. Fruits can be soaked in water, fruit juice, or appropriate liqueurs and will usually rehydrate within 1 or 2 hours, but overnight soaking may be necessary for large or whole pieces of dried foods. Overnight soaking should be done in the refrigerator. If overnight soaking is inconvenient, pour boiling water over the dried food and let stand 2 to 3 hours.

Some foods take longer to reconstitute than others. For instance, sliced carrots and potatoes require more time than green peas or beans. Rehydration is somewhat proportional to dehydration: Those pieces that take the longest to dehydrate will take the longest to rehydrate. As you dry foods take note of the slow ones, then you'll be able to allow extra time for rehydration.

Powdered, flaked, chopped, or shredded fruits and vegetables which are to be used in baking or cooking usually need no rehydration. If the pieces seem very crisp and dry, sprinkle with 1 tablespoon liquid per ½ cup of dried food. Complete rehydration for small pieces usually takes 15 to 30 minutes.

For vegetables and fruits to be used in souffles, pies, quick breads, and other dough or batters, use 2 parts liquid to 3 parts dried food. For vegetable side dishes, fruit toppings, and any other compotes which will be cooked in liquid, 1 to 1½ parts liquid to 1 part dried food is usually adequate. Extra liquid may be required for cooking.

Remember that many dried foods taste and look like fresh foods, but this is not always so. Rehydrated tomatoes, for example, do not look like fresh tomatoes in a salad, but they will make wonderful tomato sauce or can be pulverized to make tomato paste. Be creative and resourceful; an amazing smorgasbord of new recipes awaits.

Cooking

Most vegetables are cooked after they are fully rehydrated, but some, such as carrots, can be eaten raw. Vegetables can be cooked in water, broths, or vegetable juices. They can also be added dry to soups and stews which contain adequate liquid. Fruits may be cooked to make them softer or more plump for use in recipes. Fruits can be cooked in fruit juices for added flavor.

To cook, place the fruit or vegetable in a pan (do not drain off the extra liquid left from rehydration) and add enough liquid to completely cook the food. Dried fruit can be rehydrated in boiling water, then simmered 10 to 15 minutes or until tender. Rehydrated cooked fruits are sweeter than fresh fruits, so adjust the amount of sweetening agent added to recipes. When cooking vegetables, bring the liquid to a boil, then reduce the heat and allow the food to simmer until tender.

Slow cookers and microwave ovens are two additional rehydration and cooking alternatives. Place the dehydrated food and liquid in the slow cooker. Cover and cook several hours on low until food is rehydrated and tender. For microwave cooking, use 2 parts liquid to 1 part dehydrated food. Place food and liquid in a glass dish, cover, and cook 2 to 10 minutes on full power until food rehydrates. Stir occasionally. Thorough cooking may require additional time.

Drying Leftovers

Dehydrating leftovers is both easy and economical. Those leftover green beans, cooked carrots, or baked potatoes are a few of the foods that can be saved from eventual spoilage and waste. Vegetables which are generally stored and forgotten in the refrigerator can be dried and preserved before they lose their usefulness. Dehydrated leftovers can be added to soups or stews, or rehydrated and used as side dishes.

Any solid leftover food can be placed on the drying trays and dehydrated. Foods that are in sauces, for example, peas in a butter sauce, can be prepared for dehydration by draining off the excess liquid and placing the food on the drying trays. Do not dehydrate foods that are limp, spoiled, or decomposing.

Liquidlike foods, such as tomato sauce, mashed potatoes, or thick soups, can be placed on the fruit leather sheets and dried as leathers. Thick liquid foods should be dried until they are brittle. Spread the thick liquid approximately ¼ inch in thickness and ½ inch from the sides of the sheet. When dry, these waferlike foods can be broken into small pieces or powdered, and stored in airtight containers.

Check under the appropriate section in this book for the specific drying characteristics for individual foods. With leftover vegetables, a few dried herbs, and some spices you can create interesting dried soup packets for use at a later time, perhaps to take camping, backpacking, and vacationing.

Leftover pieces of cooked chicken, beef, pork, turkey, shrimp, or venison can be dehydrated. Cut the meat into ½-inch strips or cubes and place on the drying trays. Note the drying suggestions in the meat section of this book. Dehydrated pieces of cooked meat, when rehydrated, can be added to noodle or rice dishes, used in sandwich spreads, or added to sauces. Dehydrated pieces of cooked meat can be added to soups or stews without rehydrating. Add pieces of dehydrated meat along with vegetables, herbs, and spices to soup packets.

Leftover canned fruit can be drained and placed on the dehydrator trays or used to make fruit leather. Dried fruits are wonderful fast-food snacks and sweet additions to breakfast cereals, muffins, and cookies. Rehydrated fruits can be made into fruit sauces or used in your favorite dessert recipe.

Cheeses that have been ignored in the refrigerator can be dehydrated and stored before they mold. Parmesan, Romano, and provolone are excellent cheeses for drying. Slice the cheese in ¼- to ½-inch slices. Dry the cheese until it is hard. Pulverize or grate the dried cheese and store in an airtight container. Just add cheese to foods; it does not need to be rehydrated.

Even breads can be dehydrated. Whole slices of bread can be dried until hard and then pressed into bread crumbs. Breads can be cut into croutons, dried, and then stored with dried herbs to be used in stuffing.

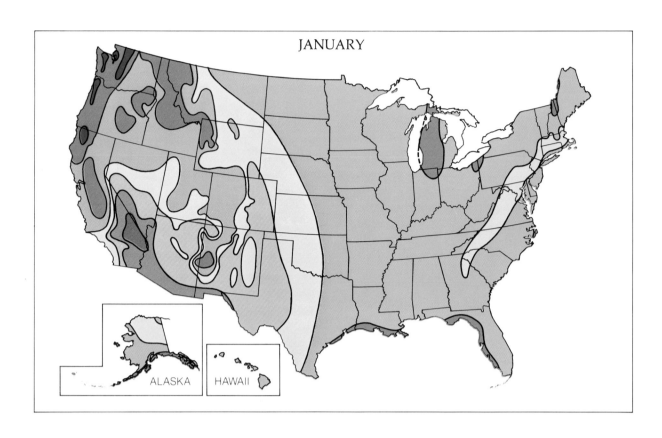

JANUARY

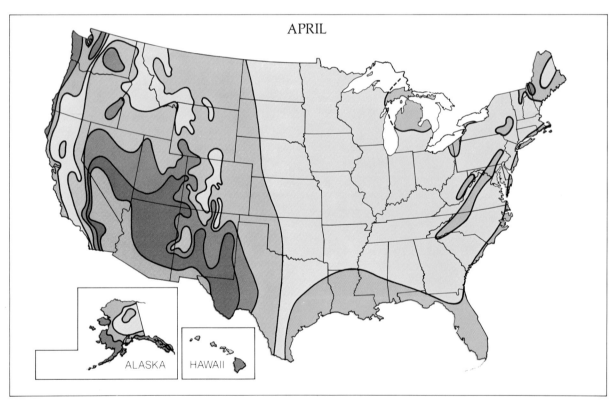

APRIL

PERCENT OF HUMIDITY

 100–91%   90–81%   80–71%   70–61%   60–51%   50–41%   40–31%   30–21%   20–11%

JULY

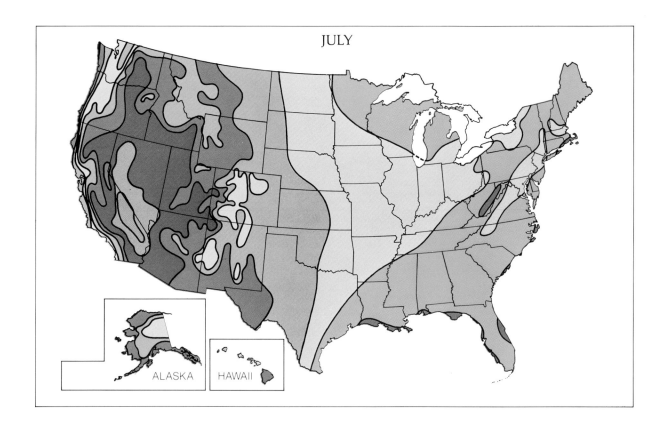

OCTOBER

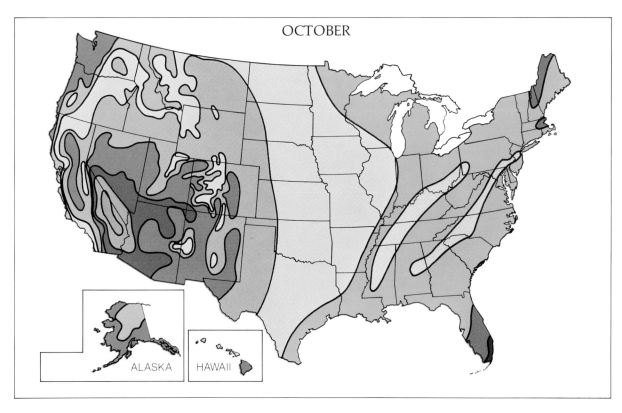

Source: The Climatic Atlas of the U.S., Environmental Data Service, U.S. Department of Commerce, June 1968.

VEGETABLES

The practice of dehydrating vegetables is attracting renewed interest. As the cost of fresh produce increases, home gardening grows in popularity. And now, thanks to the Magic Aire II Food Dehydrator, dehydrating homegrown produce is amazingly simple. Vegetables can be harvested at their prime and immediately dried, thus preserving their full flavor and nutritional value.

Dried products are as versatile as fresh. Soups, stews, omelets, souffles, croquettes, casseroles, desserts, side dishes, and vegetable chips and dips are only some of the uses for dried vegetables. Plus by dehydrating your own homegrown produce or buying vegetables in bulk during the harvest season, tremendous savings can be realized. Given below is the information you need to begin drying vegetables today.

Harvesting Suggestions

Harvest leafy vegetables, such as lettuce and spinach, early in the morning while they still glisten with dew. Pick other vegetables just before you plan to dry. If you cannot process the food immediately, store it in plastic bags or covered containers in the refrigerator or in a cool place.

Every state has extension offices from the land-grant university which should have information relative to harvesting locally grown crops. This free information will help you obtain a high-quality dried food. In the following pages of this book, suggestions are also given for harvesting foods for drying.

Preparation and Pretreatment

Wash vegetables only if necessary, as many valuable minerals and vitamins are lost by washing and soaking. Wash quickly in cold water and just before processing.

Some form of peeling, coring, slicing, or shredding is required. Specific directions are given for each vegetable. Always remove any decayed or spoiled areas. Prepare vegetables for one Magic Aire II Food Dehydrator tray or for all ten. Remember to cut vegetables into uniform sizes so all pieces will dry at the same rate.

In the following pages, directions on preparing for drying are given, including optional pretreatment procedures. Listed are suggested times for steam blanching and water-boil blanching. One of the strong arguments for dehydrating foods instead of freezing or canning is the simplicity of dehydration. Pretreatment is time-consuming, plus it causes some loss in food value. The Magic Aire II Food Dehydrator successfully dries vegetables without blanching. However, the decision is left to you. The procedure is recommended for beans, beets, corn, and potatoes. Page 7 gives additional information on pretreatment.

Drying Time

"How long does it take?" is the most commonly asked question regarding dehydration and the most difficult to answer. The drying time for vegetables ranges from 2 to 10 hours, depending on the thickness to which the food has been cut, the natural moisture content of the food, and the humidity in the air. Naturally the thicker the pieces, the longer they will take to dry. Uniform size helps to accomplish uniform drying. Foods will also dry more quickly if a greater surface area is exposed. For example, green beans which are French cut will dry more quickly than beans which are snipped. Do not overlap food on the trays as overloaded trays block air circulation and lengthen drying time. The faster the drying process, the better the color, flavor, and nutrient retention.

Check each individual vegetable for dry characteristics. Most dried vegetables are hard, crisp, leathery, or brittle. Remove vegetables as they dry. For small pieces of vegetables that may fall through the trays, use the sprouter trays or leather sheets, or collect the small pieces at the base unit. Package dehydrated vegetables in airtight containers, label and date, and preferably store in a dark place.

Rehydration

Rehydration is the process of returning moisture to the dried food product. This is accomplished by soaking vegetables in water, soup broth, or vegetable juices. Most vegetables are usually rehydrated within 1 or 2 hours. However, depending on the size of the pieces and the degree to which the food has been dried, rehydration may take as long as 8 hours. As a general rule, to rehydrate dried vegetables, soak vegetables in an equal amount of liquid. For example, rehydrate 1 cup of dried carrots in 1 cup of water or carrot juice. If the moisture is quickly absorbed, add additional liquid until the vegetables will absorb no more.

Vegetables do not need to be rehydrated before adding to soups, stews, or casseroles which contain adequate liquid. However, allow time for the vegetables to rehydrate in the liquid before cooking.

Cooking

Most rehydrated vegetables require cooking, but some, such as carrots, can be eaten immediately after rehydration. Always completely rehydrate vegetables before cooking. Not all vegetables will taste exactly like they did when fresh. Some will taste more concentrated.

To cook, place the rehydrated vegetables in a pan with any remaining rehydration liquid. If necessary, add enough additional liquid to completely cook the food. Bring the liquid and vegetables to a boil, then reduce the heat and allow the vegetables to simmer until tender. Rehydrated vegetables may also be steamed over boiling water. Season and serve vegetables while hot. Rehydrated vegetables have a bright, rich color and a good flavor.

Dried Vegetable Flakes and Powders
Vegetable flakes are made by crushing hard, dried pieces of vegetables between your hands, with a rolling pin, or in a blender. Coarsely pulverized vegetable flakes may be added to soups, breads, creamed sauces, desserts, eggs, salad dressings, and salads for extra flavor and nutrition. Label and store vegetable flakes in an airtight container.

Vegetable powders are made by placing very dry vegetable pieces in a blender or mill and pulverizing to a fine powder, or by pureeing fresh vegetables, drying as a leather until very brittle, then pulverizing. Onion, garlic, tomato, and celery are the most common vegetable powders, but any vegetable can be powdered. Use vegetable powders as a salt substitute; a nutritious seasoning; an instant soup mix; an accent to vegetables, eggs, and salads; or as a juice base.

Vegetable powder combinations are delicious. A good combination is made by using 1 teaspoon each of onion, celery, tomato, spinach, bell pepper, and carrot, along with parsley, garlic, cayenne, and rice flour. Sprinkle dry on foods to enhance flavor and nutrition, or mix 1 tablespoon of the dried vegetable mixture with 2 cups water and simmer to make a delicious broth. Vegetable powders also make excellent baby food. Simply add water, formula or milk, and season or sweeten to taste. Remember, however, that dried vegetables are very concentrated in flavor.

Vegetable Leathers
Vegetable leathers are easily made by pureeing fresh vegetables in a blender and drying on the dehydrator leather sheets. Follow the directions on page 58 for fruit leathers. Pureed tomatoes made into leather can be rehydrated and used for tomato paste, sauce, or juice. Vegetable leathers make handy foods for camping. Very dry leathers can be broken into pieces and used as vegetable chips with dips. Try vegetable combinations for new taste treats, such as tomato and onion. Season leather to taste before drying.

Vegetable Chips
When very thin slices of vegetables are dried, they result in a product much like potato chips. Vegetable chips are delicious when served with dips. Select vegetables such as tomato, cucumber, eggplant, zucchini, or parsnips. Peeling is optional. Cut very thin slices, about 1/8-inch thick, and sprinkle with salt, seasoned salts, or lemon pepper. Slices may also be marinated in barbecue sauce or soy sauce. Dry until brittle. Vegetable chips have a crunchy texture and a unique flavor.

Leftovers
The Magic Aire II Food Dehydrator can prevent the wasting of leftover fresh vegetables. Green beans, cooked carrots, fresh peas, and numerous other leftover vegetables that are generally forgotten in the refrigerator can be dried and preserved before they lose their usefulness. Dehydrated leftovers can be added to soups or stews or rehydrated and used in salads and side dishes.

Dried Vegetable Equivalents
While the following pages contain many recipes for using dried vegetables, they are intended to trigger your imagination and help you discover new ways to use dehydrated foods. Experiment with your own recipes. Look through your file for your favorite recipes which could be adapted to dried vegetables. You will need to substitute about ½ to ⅔ cup of dry vegetables for 1 cup of fresh vegetables. Rehydrate dry vegetables before using, or add additional liquid to your recipes if adding vegetables without reconstitution.

MULTI-VEGETABLE RECIPES

Winter Omelet

    4 eggs
    1/4 cup milk
    2 tablespoons bran
    1/2 teaspoon coriander
    1/2 teaspoon cumin
    1/2 teaspoon tumeric
    Salt and pepper
    1/4 cup dried tomato pieces
    1/2 cup dried chard pieces
    1 tablespoon dried onion pieces
    1/8 cup dried zucchini pieces
    1 teaspoon butter or margarine
    Grated cheese

Break eggs into a mixing bowl, add milk, and whip. Add bran, coriander, cumin, tumeric, and salt and pepper to taste. Stir in dried tomato, chard, onion, and zucchini pieces. Let mixture sit 30 minutes. Place butter or margarine in a hot, 8-inch frying pan. Pour in mixture. Reduce heat to lowest possible setting. Cover pan. Omelet is cooked when firm on top and a knife inserted in the center comes out clean, approximately 20 minutes. Before serving, sprinkle with grated cheese. Serves 2.

SUBSTITUTIONS
Small pieces of spinach, bell pepper, or mushrooms may be substituted for any of the dried vegetables.

Spaghetti Sauce

    3 cloves fresh garlic
    2 tablespoons olive oil
    1 teaspoon dried oregano
    1/2–1 teaspoon dried basil
    1 pound hamburger
    2 tablespoons dried bell pepper
    3 tablespoons dried onion
    1 dried bay leaf
    1 cup dried tomato slices
    3/4 cup dried mushroom pieces
    1 teaspoon salt
    1/2–1 teaspoon pepper
    1/2 teaspoon sugar
    18 ounces tomato paste
    4½ cups water
    2 stalks fresh celery and celery leaves, chopped
    Cooked spaghetti or noodles
    Parmesan cheese

Chop garlic and place in skillet with olive oil, dried oregano, and dried basil. Fry lightly. Add hamburger and cook until browned. Remove from heat. Add dried bell pepper, onion, bay leaf, tomato slices, mushroom pieces, plus salt, pepper, and sugar. Stir in tomato paste and water. Let sit 2 to 3 hours. Cook over medium heat until vegetables are tender, approximately 20 to 30 minutes. Add chopped celery and celery leaves 10 minutes before serving. Serve over spaghetti or noodles, and top with Parmesan cheese. Serves 4 to 6.

SUBSTITUTIONS
Four sheets of tomato leather may be used for the tomato paste, and other dried herbs may be used.

Creamed Vegetables

    2 cups dried sliced or diced vegetables*
    2½ cups boiling water
    Milk
    1/4 cup butter or margarine
    3 tablespoons flour
    1 dried bay leaf
    Salt and pepper

*Suggested vegetables to be used include beans, peas, carrots, parsnips, kohlrabi, broccoli, brussels sprouts, cauliflower, or combinations of the above.

In a medium saucepan combine dried vegetables and boiling water. Cover. Let stand 1 to 2 hours. (If desired, use cold water and reconstitute overnight in the refrigerator.) Simmer until tender, adding more liquid if necessary. Drain liquid from vegetables into a 1 cup measure. Add enough milk to make 1 cup. Melt butter or margarine in a separate saucepan. Add flour and stir until bubbly and smooth. Remove from heat. Stir in 1 cup liquid. Add bay leaf. Cook, stirring constantly, until thickened. Add drained vegetables and simmer 5 minutes. Remove bay leaf. Season to taste with salt and pepper. Serves 6.

VARIATION
Au Gratin Vegetables: Prepare Creamed Vegetables. Add 3/4 cup grated cheddar cheese and 1/4 teaspoon dry mustard. Pour into a greased 2-quart baking dish. Combine 1/2 cup dry bread crumbs and 3 tablespoons melted butter or margarine. Sprinkle over vegetables. Bake in a 350° F. oven for 30 to 35 minutes or until browned.

Bird's Vegetable Soup

1 teaspoon dried diced carrots

1 teaspoon dried garden peas

1 teaspoon dried green beans

3 teaspoons dried onion flakes

1 teaspoon dried celery

1 teaspoon dried bell pepper

1/8 cup green split peas

1/8 cup yellow split peas

1/8 cup red lentils

1/8 cup green lentils

1/8 cup brown rice

1/8 cup barley

1/8 teaspoon kelp powder

1/8 teaspoon garlic powder

1/8 teaspoon dried basil

1/8 teaspoon dried thyme

1/8 teaspoon dried parsley

1/8 teaspoon dried vegetable powder

1/8 teaspoon dulse powder

Dash of cayenne pepper

4 cups water or soup stock

Mix carrots, peas, green beans, onion flakes, celery, and bell pepper. Add split peas, lentils, brown rice, and barley. In a small bowl mix kelp powder, garlic powder, basil, thyme, parsley, vegetable broth, dulse powder, and cayenne pepper. Stir and add to other ingredients. Add water or soup stock and cook all day in a slow cooker, or let soak overnight, then cook on range for 1 hour or until vegetables are tender.

SUBSTITUTIONS

Recipe originator John Bird says that ingredients and quantities may be altered to suit individual preferences and ingredients on hand.

Oklahoma Stew

1 pound beef stew chunks

2 tablespoons oil

3 cloves fresh garlic, chopped, or 1 teaspoon dried garlic powder

6 cups water

3 tablespoons dried mushrooms

2 teaspoons dried green onions

2 tablespoons dried okra

1/2 cup dried carrots

1 cup dried tomatoes

2 cups dried potatoes

1/4 teaspoon dried basil

1/2 teaspoon salt

1/2 teaspoon pepper

Brown beef stew chunks in oil with chopped garlic or dried garlic powder. Add water and simmer 1 hour. Bring mixture to a boil, then reduce heat and add dried mushrooms, green onions, okra, carrots,

tomatoes, potatoes, basil, salt and pepper. Simmer for at least 2 hours. Taste vegetables to check tenderness. If not tender, bring to a boil and cook 10 minutes longer. Serves 4.

SUBSTITUTIONS

Green peas and/or green beans may be used in addition to or in place of the okra.

Vegetable Soup

1/2 cup dried sliced potatoes

1/4 cup dried green beans

1/4 cup dried sliced carrots

2 tablespoons dried chopped onion

4 cups water

5 dried tomato slices

3 tablespoons dried green peas

1 heaping tablespoon dried okra (optional)

1 tablespoon dried parsley

1/2 teaspoon dried thyme

1/2 teaspoon salt

1/4 teaspoon pepper

Combine dried potatoes, green beans, carrots, and onion with water in a heavy pan. Bring to a boil. Remove from heat, cover, and let stand 3 hours or overnight. Simmer 30 minutes. Add remaining vegetables and additional water if needed. Continue to cook until vegetables are tender, approximately 30 minutes. Add seasonings and simmer an additional 10 minutes. Serves 5.

VARIATIONS

Minestrone: Substitute 1/2 cup dried kidney beans, navy beans, or chick peas for the potatoes. Increase tomato slices to 10 and add 1/4 cup dried shredded cabbage and 1/2 cup dried spinach. Add 1/2 teaspoon dried oregano to remaining seasonings. Increase final cooking period to 20 minutes or until vegetables are tender. Season to taste with additional salt, pepper, and 1/2 teaspoon Worcestershire sauce. Makes about 7 cups.

Beef or Chicken Stew: Prepare Vegetable Soup as directed, adding 2 cups cubed dried beef or chicken to vegetables before soaking. Increase dried potatoes to 1½ cups. To thicken, stir together 2 tablespoons flour and 1/2 cup cold water. Add to stew, stirring constantly until thickened. Cover and simmer 5 minutes. Makes about 7 cups.

Pot Pie: Prepare Beef or Chicken Stew. Pour into a casserole dish. Prepare pastry dough for an 8-inch pie and roll to the size of the casserole dish. Transfer to dish and seal. Cut slits for steam to escape. Bake in a 400° F. oven for 30 to 35 minutes or until browned and bubbly in the center. Serves 6.

Camp Fire Soups and Stews: Prepare recipes as directed, decreasing or eliminating soaking periods, if necessary. Increase first cooking period to at least 1 hour.

Nana's Chicken Pie

1 3-4 pound chicken
Water
3 tablespoons dried onions
1/2 cup dried carrots
1/2 cup dried mushrooms
2 tablespoons dried bell pepper
1/2 cup dried parsnips
3 stalks fresh celery, diced
1½ teaspoons salt
1/2 teaspoon dried basil
1/2 teaspoon dried garlic powder
1/2 teaspoon tumeric
1 cup flour
2 rounded teaspoons baking powder
Whole milk
1/2 cup cornstarch
1/2 cup water

Cook chicken in water to cover until the meat is easily removed from the bones. Cut into 1- to 2-inch pieces. Drain and measure the liquid. Add enough water to make 8 cups. Place in a large oven-proof pan and add dried onions, carrots, mushrooms, bell pepper, and parsnips. Let soak 3 to 4 hours. Add diced celery, salt, dried basil, garlic powder, and tumeric. Cook vegetables 20 minutes or until tender, stirring occasionally. Meanwhile, to make the crust, mix the flour and baking powder. Add enough whole milk to make a stiff batter. Set aside. When vegetables are cooked, add chicken. Stir. Thicken soup with the cornstarch dissolved in 1/2 cup water. Drop the crust mixture by spoonfuls on top of the chicken and vegetables. Remove from the stove and place in a 350° F. oven until crust is brown, approximately 30 minutes. Serves 8.

SUBSTITUTIONS
Kohlrabi may be substituted for the parsnips. Tomato pieces may be added for a variation.

Vegetable Meat Loaf

1 egg
1 cup milk
1/2 teaspoon dried mustard
1/2 teaspoon Tabasco sauce
1/2 teaspoon dried garlic powder
1 teaspoon Worcestershire sauce
1/2 teaspoon dried basil
1/8 cup powdered, diced, or shredded dried carrots
2 tablespoons dried onions
2 tablespoons dried bell pepper
1/2 cup dried mushrooms
1 cup dried bread crumbs
1 pound hamburger
Ketchup

In a large bowl, beat egg and milk. Add dried mustard, Tabasco sauce, garlic powder, Worcestershire sauce, and dried basil. Mix well. Add dried carrots, onions, bell pepper, and mushrooms. Stir, then let soak 1 hour. When fully rehydrated, add dried bread crumbs and hamburger. Mix all ingredients and shape into a loaf. Top with a stream of ketchup and bake approximately 1 hour in a 350° F. oven. Serves 4 to 6.

SUBSTITUTIONS
Dried tomato pieces may be added, and small pieces of any dried vegetable may be substituted for the carrots.

Swiss-Style Vegetable Soup

1 pound beef stew cubes
6 cups water
1 dried bay leaf
1 teaspoon salt
1/2 teaspoon pepper
3/4 cup dried tomato powder
2 tablespoons powdered dry milk
1/3 cup dried onions
1/3 cup dried bell pepper
1/3 cup dried garden peas
1/2 cup dried mushroom pieces
1 teaspoon dried oregano
1 teaspoon dried garlic powder
1 teaspoon sugar
1/2 teaspoon dried basil
4 cups water
4 stalks fresh celery, chopped
4 tablespoons flour
1/2 cup water
Cooked noodles

Cook beef stew cubes in 6 cups water with bay leaf, salt and pepper for 1 to 1½ hours. Add dried tomato powder, powdered dry milk, dried onions, bell pepper, garden peas, mushroom pieces, oregano, garlic powder, sugar, basil, and 4 cups water. Stir. Remove from heat and let sit 2 to 3 hours. Bring to a boil. Add chopped fresh celery. Cook until vegetables are tender, approximately 30 minutes. Thicken by combining the flour and 1/2 cup water. Serve over cooked noodles. Serves 4 to 6.

SUBSTITUTIONS
Two to three sheets of tomato leather may be substituted for the tomato powder. Small pieces of green beans may be used in place of the peas. Carrots and zucchini may be added.

ASPARAGUS

GENERAL INFORMATION

Water content of fresh food:
92%.

Selection of fresh food for drying:
Choose young, tender stalks of asparagus with compact tips and rounded spears. Asparagus may be either green or white. If harvesting asparagus, select spears which are 6 to 8 inches, and cut at the soil line. The fresher the asparagus, the better the dried product.

Preparation for drying:
Remove the woody end of the asparagus stalk, which will become tough and stringy when dried, plus any limp, rotting, or moldy pieces. Do not wash until immediately before placing on the dehydrator trays, as water encourages the loss of nutrients and accelerates deterioration. Never soak asparagus. Slice diagonally into ½-inch pieces, or cut into ½-inch cubes.

Optional pretreatment:
Steam blanch 3 to 5 minutes, or water boil small stalks 2 minutes and large stalks 4 minutes.

Characteristics of dried product:
Crisp and brittle.

Ways to use:
Large pieces of asparagus stem do not rehydrate well. Pulverize in the blender and add to salad dressings or sprinkle on salads.

Rehydrate asparagus spears and add to fancy sauces, soups, stews, souffles, and casseroles.

RECIPE SUGGESTIONS

Cream of Asparagus Soup
    1 cup dried asparagus pieces
    4 cups water
    1 large or 2 small fresh potatoes
    2 tablespoons butter or margarine
    1 teaspoon dried basil
    1 teaspoon dried garlic powder
    2 tablespoons flour
    4 cups milk
    Salt and pepper
    Parmesan cheese

In a large saucepan soak dried asparagus pieces in water for 30 minutes. Add potatoes which have been peeled and cut into chunks, and boil until potatoes are tender. Add butter or margarine, dried basil, and dried garlic powder. Pour entire mixture into blender and puree. Add flour and blend again.

Return soup to pan and add milk. Cook over medium heat until hot and thickened. Salt and pepper to taste. Sprinkle with Parmesan cheese before serving. Serves 6 to 8.

SUBSTITUTIONS
Dehydrated potatoes may be used in place of fresh potatoes. Reconstitute with asparagus, adding approximately 1 cup more water. Cream of tomato, zucchini, or cauliflower soup may be prepared in the same manner.

Asparagus Omelet
    1/2 cup dried asparagus pieces
    1/2 cup water
    2 teaspoons lemon juice
    8 eggs
    1/2 cup milk
    Salt and pepper
    Grated cheese

Place dried asparagus pieces in water and lemon juice. Refrigerate 8 hours. To prepare omelet, beat eggs and add milk. Salt and pepper to taste. Pour one-fourth of the mixture into a heated and slightly greased omelet pan. Rotate until the egg evenly covers the bottom of the pan, and cook until the egg sets. Place one-fourth of the asparagus filling in the center of the omelet and fold over. Repeat with remaining ingredients. Top with grated cheese before serving. Serves 4.

VARIATION
Creamed Asparagus and Tuna: Prepare asparagus filling as directed. Mix with 1 10¾-ounce can cream of mushroom soup. Add 1 6½-ounce can tuna. Thin with milk if desired. Heat through and serve over hot buttered toast.

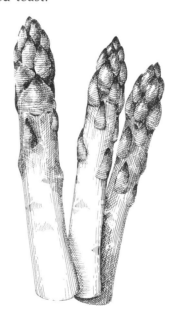

BEANS

GREEN OR YELLOW

GENERAL INFORMATION

Water content of fresh food:
90%.

Selection of fresh food for drying:
Choose brightly colored beans that are young and tender, firm and crisp. Beans should snap easily when bent. Avoid discolored, limp, bulging, or rusted beans. Old pods become discolored, leathery, and stringy, with mealy beans inside.

Preparation for drying:
Wash beans and snip off both ends. Pull off any strings. Beans may be dried whole, French cut, or diagonally sliced into ½-inch pieces. The more surface area exposed, the quicker the beans will dry.

Pretreatment:
Steam blanch 12 minutes, or water boil 8 minutes. Pretreatment produces a more tender product and reduces rehydration time.

Characteristics of dried product:
Brittle.

Ways to use:
Add to soups or stews, allowing time for rehydration.

Rehydrate and add to casseroles, sauces, or salads.

Rehydrate, cook, and serve as a vegetable dish.

RECIPE SUGGESTIONS

Green Bean Dip

1/2 cup dried green beans

1/2 cup water

1/4 cup oil

1/2 cup grated or diced sharp Cheddar or Swiss cheese

2 tablespoons chopped fresh parsley, basil, or watercress

2 cloves garlic, minced

Cayenne pepper

Soak dried green beans in water for 2 to 4 hours or until squeezable. Place beans, any remaining rehydration water, and oil in the blender and puree. Add half the cheese plus the fresh herbs, minced garlic, and a pinch of cayenne pepper. Blend. Add remaining cheese and blend again. Refrigerate at least 1 hour, preferably overnight. (Serve with chips, crackers, or pieces of whole wheat pita bread. May also be used as a sandwich spread.)

Creamed Green Beans

1 cup dried green beans

2 cups water

1 10¾-ounce can cream of asparagus or mushroom soup

Salt and pepper

Boiled potatoes

Soak dried green beans in water for 8 hours or overnight. Cook over medium heat until tender. Add soup. Stir and cook slowly until mixture has a saucelike consistency. Season to taste with salt and pepper. Serve over boiled potatoes. Serves 4.

BEETS

GENERAL INFORMATION

Water content of fresh food:
87%.

Selection of fresh food for drying:
Beets with a deep red color and firm texture are best for drying. Avoid beets that are soft, woody, or have tough scales.

Preparation for drying:
Trim beet greens, leaving roots and 2 inches of tops to prevent bleeding. (Beet greens may also be dried. See Swiss Chard for drying instructions.) Boil beets until the skins slip off easily, approximately 15 minutes. Cool. Trim crown and root ends, and peel off skin. Cut into ¼- to ½-inch slices, ½-inch cubes, or ¼-inch shoestring strips.

Pretreatment:
Boil 15 minutes as described above.

Characteristics of dried product:
Hard.

Ways to use:
Rehydrate, cook, and use in recipes calling for beets.

Rehydrate, cook, and serve with melted butter as a side dish.

Pulverize to make beet powder.

Pulverize and add to salads and salad dressings.

Pulverize and use as a sweetener. Beets tend to sweeten when dried because of their high sugar content.

Add pulverized beets to beverages to increase iron content.

RECIPE SUGGESTIONS

Maggie's Beet Jelly

1 cup dried beet pieces

3 cups water

1 .24-ounce package unsweetened grape Kool-Aid

1 1¾-ounce package Sure-Jell

4½ cups sugar

Soak dried beets in water for 3 hours. Place beets and water in blender and puree. Measure puree and add enough water to make 4 cups. Pour into a large pan. Add Kool-Aid and Sure-Jell. Stir. Bring mixture to a boil. Stir in sugar. Return mixture to a rolling boil and cook 4 minutes. Remove from heat. Pour into small sterile jars and seal. Makes about 54 ounces.

Borscht

3 cups dried beet slices

8 cups water

1 cup lemon juice

1/4 cup honey

1 teaspoon salt

1 teaspoon dried dill weed (optional)

2 eggs, beaten

Sour cream or yogurt

Shredded hard-boiled eggs

Place dried beet slices in 6 cups water in a large pot. Soak for 30 minutes. Transfer half of the beets and liquid to a blender and pulverize to very small pieces. Repeat with remaining beets and liquid. Return mixture to pot. Place the additional 2 cups water in blender and blend to loosen remaining beet puree. Add to mixture in pot. Cover and simmer slowly for about 30 minutes or until beets are soft. Remove from heat and add lemon juice, honey, salt, and dill. Cool to lukewarm. Vigorously stir in beaten eggs. Refrigerate until well chilled or overnight. To serve, top with sour cream or yogurt and shredded hard-boiled eggs. Makes 9 cups.

BROCCOLI

GENERAL INFORMATION

Water content of fresh food:
89%.

Selection of fresh food for drying:
Both the stalks and flowerets of fresh broccoli may be dried. Harvest broccoli when the flower head is fully developed but before individual flower buds start to open. Cut the stalk 6 to 7 inches below the flower head. The stalks and stem branches should be tender and firm with fresh leaves. Avoid broccoli with yellowing bud clusters and woody stalks.

Preparation for drying:
Wash briefly in cold water, but do not soak unless necessary to remove insects. Remove any woody or blemished areas. Cut stalks in halves or quarters not more than ⅜-inch thick. Break the flower heads into small, uniform pieces.

Optional pretreatment:
Soak broccoli in a solution of 2 tablespoons salt and 1/2 gallon cold water for 15 to 30 minutes. Steam blanch 5 minutes, or water boil 3 minutes.

Characteristics of dried product:
Brittle.

Ways to use:
Rehydrate broccoli flowerets, cook, and serve as a side dish.

Add flowerets and small pieces of broccoli stems to soups and stews.

Broccoli stems tend to be tough. Pulverize and use as vegetable flakes on salads or add to casseroles and sauces.

RECIPE SUGGESTION

Broccoli Quiche

1/2 cup dried broccoli pieces

1/2 cup milk

1/2 cup sour cream

3 eggs, beaten

1 cup grated Swiss cheese

1/4 cup chopped onion

1/4 teaspoon salt

1/8 teaspoon pepper

1 9-inch unbaked pie shell (recipe at right)

1/4 cup fried bacon pieces

Soak dried broccoli pieces in milk for 1 hour. Stir in sour cream. Add beaten eggs, grated cheese, chopped onion, salt and pepper. Mix. Pour into unbaked pie shell. Bake in a 375° F. oven for 35 to 40 minutes or until a knife inserted in the center comes out clean. Top with fried bacon pieces. Serves 6.

SUBSITIONS
Other vegetables such as spinach, zucchini, and cauliflower, or combinations including tomato, mushrooms, bell pepper, or celery may be substituted for the broccoli.

Pie Pastry
    3 cups flour
    1 teaspoon salt
    1 1/8 cups lard or shortening
    5 tablespoons water
    1 teaspoon vinegar
    1 egg

Blend together flour, salt, and lard or shortening. In a small bowl mix water, vinegar, and egg. Pour over dry mixture and mix. Makes 4 single-crust or 2 double-crust pies. Unused pastry may be stored in the refrigerator or frozen.

BRUSSELS SPROUTS

GENERAL INFORMATION

Water content of fresh food:
85%.

Selection of fresh food for drying:
Select firm, compact, bright green sprouts. Home-grown sprouts are ready to harvest when they are firm and solid. Harvest from the base of the plant first, then work up the stalk. Brussels sprouts are not suitable for drying if sprouts are soft or if the leaves have turned yellow.

Preparation for drying:
Remove coarse outer leaves and trim stem ends. Wash in cold water. Cut in half lengthwise or chop into smaller pieces. The core may be removed for quicker drying.

Optional pretreatment:
Steam blanch small heads 3 minutes, large heads 5 minutes, or water boil 2 to 3 minutes.

Characteristics of dried product:
Crispy.

Ways to use:
Add brussels sprouts to soups, stews, or casseroles.

Rehydrate and add to cheese sauces or cream soups.

Pulverize and use as a seasoning.

Rehydrate, cook, butter, and serve as a vegetable dish.

Marinate small pieces and add to salads.

RECIPE SUGGESTION

Golden Brussels Sprouts
    1 heaping cup dried brussels sprout halves
    1 cup water
    2 tablespoons melted butter or margarine
    1 egg, beaten
    2 tablespoons dry bread crumbs
    Salt and pepper

Soak dried brussels sprouts in water in a small frying pan for 2 hours. Cover and simmer until tender. Drain. Pour melted butter or margarine, beaten egg, and bread crumbs over brussels sprouts and toss gently. Fry over medium heat until golden brown. Season to taste with salt and pepper. Serves 4.

CABBAGE

GENERAL INFORMATION

Water content of fresh food:
92%.

Selection of fresh food for drying:
Both green and red cabbage can be successfully dried. Select fresh firm heads that are heavy for their size.

Preparation for drying:
Trim outer leaves that are wilted or brown. Cut in half and remove core. Core becomes very tough when dried. Cut into ½- to 1-inch strips, or dry whole leaves.

Optional pretreatment:
Steam blanch 4 to 5 minutes, or water boil 3 minutes.

Characteristics of dried product:
Brittle.

Ways to use:
Add to soups or stews. Cabbage is especially good in soups with ham and root vegetables.

Pulverize and use as vegetable flakes in salads.

Rehydrate, cook, season with butter and caraway seeds, and serve as a side dish.

RECIPE SUGGESTION

Cabbage-Hamburger Casserole

2 cups dried green cabbage strips
4 cups water
1 pound hamburger
1 medium onion, chopped
1 teaspoon dried garlic powder
1 teaspoon dried basil
2-3 cups uncooked noodles
1 10¾-ounce can cream of mushroom soup
Salt and pepper
Mozzarella cheese

Soak dried green cabbage strips in water in a large pan for 15 to 30 minutes. Meanwhile, fry hamburger, chopped onion, garlic powder, and dried basil over medium heat until browned. Drain grease. Add noodles to cabbage and cook until noodles are soft and cabbage becomes transparent, approximately 10 to 15 minutes. Drain mixture, saving liquid, and add cabbage and noodles to hamburger. Mix liquid with cream of mushroom soup and add to casserole mixture. Stir. Salt and pepper to taste. Pour into a large casserole dish and top with grated mozzarella cheese. Cover and bake in a 350° F. oven for 30 minutes. Serves 6.

CARROTS

GENERAL INFORMATION

Water content of fresh food:
88%.

Selection of fresh food for drying:
For best results, use crisp carrots. Carrots that are limp, shriveled, woody, or have a pithy core should not be dried.

Preparation for drying:
Remove tops and stringy ends. Wash, and peel if desired. Cut crosswise, lengthwise, or diagonally into ⅜-inch slices, cube, or coarsely grate.

Optional pretreatment:
Steam blanch small pieces 2 to 3 minutes, larger pieces 5 to 7 minutes, or water boil 2 to 4 minutes.

Characteristics of dried product:
Tough to brittle.

Ways to use:
Pulverize and add to orange juice.

Rehydrate, cook, season with butter and herbs, and serve as a side dish.

Use in soups, stews, casseroles, breads, and cookies.

Pulverize carrots and use to make baby food, or sprinkle as vegetable flakes over salads.

RECIPE SUGGESTIONS

Spicy Carrot Cookies

1 cup dried grated carrots
1/2 cup hot water
3/4 cup butter or margarine
1 cup firmly packed brown sugar
1 egg
2 tablespoons water
1 teaspoon vanilla
1¾ cups flour
1 teaspoon salt
1/2 teaspoon baking soda
1/2 teaspoon cinnamon
1/4 teaspoon nutmeg

Combine dried grated carrots and 1/2 cup hot water. Let sit 30 minutes, stirring twice. Beat together butter or margarine, brown sugar, egg, 2 tablespoons water, and vanilla until creamy. Stir together flour, salt, baking soda, cinnamon, and nutmeg. Add to creamed mixture. Fold in carrots. Drop by teaspoonfuls onto slightly greased baking sheets. Bake in a 350° F. oven for 15 to 18 minutes or until lightly browned. Yields about 4 dozen.

Spicy Carrot Cookies for a nutritious after-school snack

Carrot Cake

1 cup coarsely pulverized or grated dried carrots

1 cup water

4 eggs

1½ cups butter or margarine

1 cup white flour

1 cup whole wheat flour

1/2 cup white sugar

1/2 cup firmly packed brown sugar

1 teaspoon baking powder

1 teaspoon baking soda

1 teaspoon salt

4 tablespoons bran (optional)

1 teaspoon coriander (optional)

2 teaspoons cinnamon

1 cup raisins

1 cup chopped walnuts

Apple-Orange Frosting (page 73)

Soak coarsely pulverized or grated dried carrots in water for 30 minutes. Drain any remaining liquid. In a small bowl beat together eggs and butter or margarine. In a large bowl mix white flour, whole wheat flour, white sugar, brown sugar, baking powder, baking soda, salt, bran, coriander, and cinnamon. Add creamed mixture and beat until smooth. Stir raisins and chopped walnuts into the carrot mixture, then add to the batter. Let the batter sit for 10 minutes. Preheat oven to 350° F. Grease and flour two 9-inch round cake pans, a 10-inch tube pan, or a 9-by-13-inch rectangular pan. Bake 40 to 45 minutes, depending on pan size, or until toothpick inserted in center comes out clean. Let cool. Frost with Apple-Orange Frosting.

CAULIFLOWER

GENERAL INFORMATION

Water content of fresh food:

91%.

Selection of fresh food for drying:

Choose fresh, solid heads which are white, smooth, and compact. Do not use cauliflower which has darkened or is rough in appearance or coarse in texture.

Preparation for drying:

Separate the leaves from the cauliflower head. Cut off the woody base. Separate into very small flowerets or slice or cube larger flowerets into ½- to 1-inch pieces.

Optional pretreatment:

Steam blanch 4 to 6 minutes, or water boil 2 to 4 minutes.

Characteristics of dried product:

Hard and crisp.

Ways to use:

Add to soups or vegetable stews.

Rehydrate and add to casserole dishes and eggs, or cook and use as a side dish with herb butter.

Rehydrate and add to cream and cheese sauces.

Pulverize and add flakes to salads.

RECIPE SUGGESTION

Cauliflower Crepes

1 cup very small dried cauliflower pieces

1½ cups water

2 tablespoons butter or margarine

1/4 teaspoon salt

Pepper

1/4 cup dried celery powder

2 tablespoons flour

1 cup milk

1/2 cup sour cream

8-10 crepes (recipe at right)

Cheese sauce (recipe at right)

In a medium saucepan soak dried cauliflower pieces in water for 15 minutes. Cook rehydrated cauliflower over medium heat until soft, adding more cooking water if necessary. When tender, drain excess water. Add butter or margarine, salt, pepper to taste, and dried celery powder. Stir. Sprinkle flour over the cauliflower mixture. Stir gently. Add milk and cook until thickened, stirring constantly. Remove from heat. Stir in sour cream and heat through. Place 2 to 3 tablespoons mixture in each crepe and roll. Pour warm cheese sauce over crepes.

SUBSTITUTIONS

Small pieces of broccoli, zucchini, asparagus, or spinach may be used in place of the cauliflower. Dried onion and dried herbs may be added for additional flavor.

Crepes

1 cup milk
2 tablespoons melted butter or margarine
2 eggs
3/4 cup flour

Blend milk, melted butter or margarine, and eggs in blender. Add flour and blend until smooth. For more tender crepes, refrigerate batter for at least 2 hours before baking. Pour 1/8 cup of batter into a lightly greased and preheated 6-inch frying pan, rotating the pan until the batter covers the bottom surface. Turn over when lightly browned on the edges. Crepes may also be prepared with any crepe cooker. Leftover crepes may be stored in the refrigerator or layered between waxed paper and frozen.

Cheese Sauce

2 tablespoons butter or margarine
2 tablespoons flour
1 cup milk
3/4 cup grated sharp Cheddar cheese
Salt and pepper

Melt butter or margarine in a small saucepan. Stir in flour and cook gently for 2 to 3 minutes. Add milk and cook until sauce has thickened. Add cheese and stir until cheese melts. Season to taste with salt and pepper.

CELERY

GENERAL INFORMATION

Water content of fresh food:
94%.

Selection of fresh food for drying:
Use fresh, crisp stalks that are brittle enough to snap when bent. Limp, yellowing, or wilted celery results in an unsatisfactory dried product. Both green and white celery may be dried.

Preparation for drying:
Trim off roots and peel coarse strings. Remove any brown or woody areas. Wash stalks and leaves. (Leaves may be dried, crushed, and used for seasoning.) Slice celery crosswise or lengthwise into ¼-inch strips or pieces.

Optional pretreatment:
Steam blanch 2 to 3 minutes, or water boil 1 to 2 minutes.

Characteristics of dried product:
Hard.

Ways to use:
Use in cooking. Celery does not rehydrate crisp enough to enjoy as a raw vegetable.

Add to dry soup mixes.

Add to stews, meats, and soups.

Pulverize pieces and leaves and use as vegetable flakes in salads.

Make celery vinegar for use in salad dressings by adding celery pieces to white vinegar and allowing to sit 2 weeks.

RECIPE SUGGESTIONS

Celery Salt

1/2 cup pulverized dried celery
1/2 cup salt

Mix pulverized dried celery and salt. Store in an airtight container.

Cream of Celery Soup

1½ cups chicken stock or 1 10¾-ounce can chicken broth

1/2 cup dried celery pieces

1/4 cup dried onion pieces

3 tablespoons flour

1 cup water

1 cup milk

2 tablespoons butter or margarine

1/4 teaspoon pepper

Dry mustard

Parmesan cheese (optional)

Place chicken stock or broth in a large saucepan. Add dried celery and onion pieces. Let sit 30 minutes. Cook over medium heat until vegetables are tender. Place in a blender and puree. Add flour, water, and milk. Blend thoroughly. Return to saucepan. Add butter or margarine, pepper, and a pinch of dry mustard. Cook over medium heat until soup thickens, stirring often. If desired, sprinkle with Parmesan cheese before servings. Makes 5 cups.

SUBSTITUTIONS

Asparagus, cauliflower, and zucchini, or combinations such as tomato-zucchini or broccoli-cauliflower may be used in place of the celery.

CORN

GENERAL INFORMATION

Water content of fresh food:
73%.

Selection of fresh food for drying:
Both yellow and white sweet corn can be dried. Select young, tender ears with green husks and dark brown silk. The kernels should be touching one another with no space in between. Kernels are plump with milk juice when ears are ripe. Field corn can also be dried, but use is restricted to grinding for cornmeal.

Preparation for drying:
Process corn as soon as possible after picking as the sugar quickly turns to starch. Remove the outer husk and silk. Cut away any worm damage. Place cobs in rapidly boiling water for 5 minutes, or steam blanch for 8 minutes. Plunge immediately into cold water. When cool, drain. Cut kernels from cob. Spread on sprouter trays, leather sheets, or cheesecloth as small pieces may fall through the dehydrator trays.

Pretreatment:
Steam blanch on the cob 8 minutes, or water boil 5 minutes, as described above.

Characteristics of dried product:
Hard.

Ways to use:
Corn can be successfully rehydrated in milk for use in creamed dishes.

Use in soups, casseroles, chowders, and stews.

Pulverize and use for corn flour or cornmeal.

RECIPE SUGGESTIONS

Corn Chips
An alternative drying procedure.

2 cups cut fresh corn

1/4 tablespoon dried onion powder

1/4 teaspoon dried garlic powder

Salt

3 tablespoons chopped fresh green bell pepper

3 tablespoons chopped fresh tomato

Puree corn, onion powder, garlic powder, and a dash of salt in blender. Pour onto leather sheets. Sprinkle with chopped bell pepper and tomato. Dry until crispy and crinkled. Break into chips.

Francie's Sweet Corn Bread

1 cup dried corn

1¾ cups flour

2 teaspoons baking powder

1½ teaspoons salt

3/4 cup sugar

2 eggs, beaten

1½ cups evaporated milk

1/2 cup oil

Grind dried corn in the Magic Mill. Measure 3/4 cup cornmeal. In a mixing bowl combine cornmeal, flour, baking powder, salt, and sugar. Beat together eggs, evaporated milk, and oil. Add to dry mixture, stirring only enough to mix. Pour into a greased 9-by-13-inch baking pan. Bake in a 350° F. oven for 30 minutes or until edges turn brown. Serves 12.

Creamed Corn

1 cup dried corn

2 cups milk

1/2 teaspoon salt

1/4 teaspoon pepper

1 teaspoon sugar

2 tablespoons butter or margarine

Toast or English muffins

In a medium saucepan combine dried corn, milk, salt, pepper, and sugar. Let soak until corn has absorbed at least half of the liquid, approximately 4 hours. When rehydrated, add butter or margarine and cook over medium heat until kernels are tender and the corn mixture has thickened, about 10 minutes. Serve over hot buttered toast or English muffins. Serves 4.

Tender and tasty Francie's Sweet Corn Bread

CUCUMBERS

GENERAL INFORMATION

Water content of fresh food:
95%.

Selection of fresh food for drying:
Pick cucumbers with dark green skins. The flesh should be white and the seeds small and soft. Old cucumbers are dull in color, soft in texture, and have large seeds, rendering them unacceptable for drying.

Preparation for drying:
Peel the cucumber skin because it becomes tough and bitter when dried. Slice into ¼- to ½-inch pieces or shred. Slices may be sprinkled with seasoned salt before drying for use as chips.

Characteristics of dried product:
Brittle.

Ways to use:
Serve dried slices as vegetable chips with dips.

Pulverize and use as vegetable flakes in salads or add to salad dressings.

Rehydrate, dip in beaten egg, roll in bread crumbs, then deep-fat fry.

Rehydrate small pieces and cook 3 to 5 minutes. Serve with lemon juice or herbs.

Pulverize and add to jello salads.

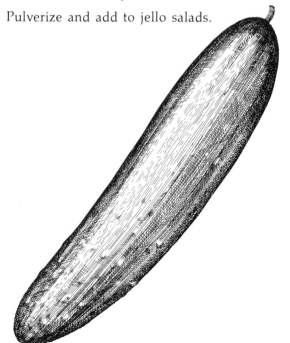

RECIPE SUGGESTIONS

Cucumber Dip (Pictured on page 44)

1/2 cup coarsely pulverized dried cucumber
6 ounces cream cheese, softened
2 tablespoons sour cream
1 tablespoon mayonnaise
1 teaspoon dried dill
Salt and pepper
Chips

Mix all ingredients, salt and pepper to taste, and refrigerate until well chilled. (Serve with chips, or use as a sandwich spread.) Makes 1 cup.

VARIATIONS

Alfalfa sprouts, chopped tomatoes, or grated Monterey Jack cheese may be added for variety.

Cucumber Muffins

1 cup coarsely pulverized dried cucumber
1½ cups water
2 cups flour
2 teaspoons baking soda
1 teaspoon baking powder
1 teaspoon salt
3 teaspoons cinnamon
1 cup oil or melted butter
3 eggs, beaten
1½ cups sugar
2 teaspoons vanilla
1/3 cup raisins
1/3 cup sunflower seeds or chopped nuts
Sesame seeds
Melted butter

Combine cucumber flakes and water in a small bowl. Let sit 30 minutes to rehydrate. In a large bowl mix flour, baking soda, baking powder, salt, and cinnamon. When the cucumbers have rehydrated, add oil or melted butter, beaten eggs, sugar, and vanilla. Add to dry ingredients. Stir just until moistened. Fold in raisins and seeds or nuts. Grease 24 to 30 muffin cups and fill half full. Sprinkle with sesame seeds. Bake in a 350° F. oven for 25 minutes or until done. Brush with melted butter while still hot and serve.

EGGPLANT

GENERAL INFORMATION

Water content of fresh food:
92%.

Selection of fresh food for drying:
Select fresh, firm, pear-shaped eggplants which are heavy in relation to their size. Avoid eggplants that are dull in color or soft and seedy. Check for damaged areas on the smooth purple skin.

Preparation for drying:
Trim off the stem and peel the eggplant. (Peels may be dried separately.) Cut into ¼- to ½-inch round slices, julienne strips, or ½-inch cubes.

Optional pretreatment:
Steam blanch 3 to 4 minutes, or water boil 1 to 2 minutes.

Characteristics of dried product:
Waferlike yet brittle.

Ways to use:
Pulverize dried peels and use as a garnish on eggplant dishes or add to salad dressings.

Rehydrate and add to tomato dishes, use with eggs, or add to sauces.

RECIPE SUGGESTIONS

Eggplant Dip
1 cup dried eggplant pieces
1 cup water
8 ounces yogurt
1 clove garlic, minced
1 lemon, juiced
Crushed dried mint or parsley

Place dried eggplant pieces in a small pan with water. Let sit 1 hour, then simmer until water evaporates. Place yogurt, minced garlic, and lemon juice in blender. Blend lightly. Add cooked eggplant and blend thoroughly. Refrigerate until well chilled. Garnish with crushed dried mint or parsley. (Serve as a dip with pita bread pieces or dehydrated vegetable slices, or stuff cherry tomatoes and use as an hors d'oeuvre.)

Eggplant Parmesan (Pictured on page 36)
18-24 dried eggplant slices
4-6 cups water
24 ounces tomato paste
3 eggs, beaten
1-1½ cups dry bread crumbs
3-4 teaspoons vegetable oil
3-4 teaspoons olive oil
4-6 tablespoons dried oregano
6 ounces grated Parmesan cheese
12 ounces shredded mozzarella cheese

Soak dried eggplant slices in water for 20 to 30 minutes. Rotate every 5 minutes so slices are continually moist and rehydrate evenly. Remove eggplant from water and save water. Mix tomato paste with 1 to 2 cups of the water until paste resembles the consistency of tomato sauce. Dip both sides of rehydrated eggplant in beaten egg, then coat with bread crumbs. Fry over medium heat in vegetable oil and olive oil. Brown both sides. In a 9-by-13-inch pan, layer one-third of the eggplant, tomato paste, dried oregano, Parmesan cheese, and mozzarella cheese. Repeat twice. Let mixture sit 1 to 2 hours before baking. Cover pan with aluminum foil and bake in a 350° F. oven for 35 minutes. Remove aluminum foil and bake for an additional 10 minutes. Cool at least 10 minutes before serving. Serves 6 to 8.

SUBSTITUTION
The tomato paste may be made by combining the reserved liquid with tomato leather sheets.

KOHLRABI

Water content of fresh food:
90%.

Selection of fresh food for drying:
Kohlrabi, also known as cabbage-turnip, is a round, globe-shaped vegetable which forms as a swelling at the base of the plant. Harvest when 2 to 3 inches in diameter. Both green and purple varieties can be dried.

Preparation for drying:
Remove leaves, tops, and roots. Cut into ¼- to ½-inch slices or cubes and dry with or without pretreatment, or steam or water blanch whole globes without peeling until tender, then cool, slip off skin, and slice or cube.

Optional pretreatment:
Steam blanch whole globes 3 minutes, cubes 1 minute, or water boil 1 to 2 minutes.

Characteristics of dried product:
Brittle.

Ways to use:
Rehydrate, cook, and serve as a vegetable with butter and seasonings.

Rehydrate small pieces and add to mixed salads.

RECIPE SUGGESTION

Creamed Kohlrabi

1½-2 cups dried kohlrabi slices
1 dried bay leaf
1 small onion studded with 4-6 whole cloves
Water
2 tablespoons butter or margarine
2 tablespoons flour
1 cup milk
Nutmeg

In a medium saucepan soak dried kohlrabi, bay leaf, and clove-studded onion in enough water to cover for 2 hours. Cook until tender. Meanwhile, make a white sauce by melting butter or margarine in a small sauce pan. Stir in flour and cook gently 2 to 3 minutes. Add milk and cook until thickened. When kohlrabi is tender, drain remaining water and remove bay leaf and onion. Pour white sauce over vegetables and sprinkle with nutmeg before serving. Serves 4.

SUBSTITUTION
Parsnips may be used in place of the kohlrabi.

LETTUCE

GENERAL INFORMATION

Water content of fresh food:
95%.

Selection of fresh food for drying:
Any variety of lettuce can be dried. Choose fresh lettuce with tender, crisp leaves. Avoid lettuce that is wilted or rusted.

Preparation for drying:
Dust or wash. For lettuce varieties with a prominent vein, such as romaine, fold each individual leaf lengthwise along the vein and cut out the vein with kitchen scissors.

Characteristics of dried product:
Easily crushable.

Ways to use:
Coarsely pulverize and sprinkle on salads for extra flavor.

Pulverize and use in salad dressings.

RECIPE SUGGESTION

Lettuce Soup

1 cup small dried lettuce pieces
1 cup water
2 cups chicken broth
2 tablespoons butter
1/4 teaspoon nutmeg
1 small onion, grated
2 tablespoons flour
1 cup water
Grated cheese

Soak dried lettuce in 1 cup water and chicken broth for 1 hour. Puree in blender, then strain. Discard pulp. Add butter, nutmeg, and grated onion. Mix together until smooth the flour and remaining 1 cup water. Add to soup. Cook over medium heat until soup thickens and butter melts. Top with grated cheese before serving. Makes 4 cups.

LIMA BEANS

GENERAL INFORMATION

Water content of fresh food:
68%.

Selection of fresh food for drying:
Choose fresh, young, firm, and well-filled but not bulging pods. Pods should be crisp and unblemished. Beans with a hard or tough skin are over mature and will lack flavor.

Preparation for drying:
Remove the beans from the pods. Wash if necessary.

Optional pretreatment:
Steam blanch small beans 3 minutes, large beans 6 minutes, or water boil 2 to 4 minutes.

Characteristics of dried product:
Very hard.

Ways to use:
Add dry to soups or stews.

Rehydrate, cook, and use as a vegetable dish, or add to casseroles.

RECIPE SUGGESTIONS

Lima Bean Medley

1 cup dried lima beans

2 cups water

1 tablespoon chopped fresh onion

1 cup sliced fresh carrots

1/4 teaspoon ginger

5 strips bacon

In a large saucepan soak dried lima beans in water for 8 hours. Add additional water during soaking time if necessary. When beans are rehydrated, add chopped onion, sliced carrots, and ginger. Simmer over medium heat until vegetables are tender. While vegetables are cooking, fry bacon until crisp. Drain and crumble into 1-inch pieces. Drain liquid from cooked vegetables, stir in bacon, and serve. Serves 6.

Lima Beans in Sour Cream

1½ cups dried lima beans

Water

2/3 cup sour cream

Salt

In a medium saucepan soak lima beans in water to cover for 8 hours. Cover pan and simmer until tender. Drain any remaining water. Add sour cream and salt to taste. Heat through and serve warm. Serves 4.

MUSHROOMS

GENERAL INFORMATION

Water content of fresh food:
90%.

Selection of fresh food for drying:
Any edible variety of mushroom can be dried. Select blemish-free mushrooms with firm flesh. The cap should be firmly attached to the stem. Shriveled caps indicate a lack of freshness.

Preparation for drying:
Cut off the woody base of the stem. Wipe mushrooms clean with a damp cloth, never soak. Cut into ½-inch cubes, or slice. Caps and stems may be separated. Small mushrooms can be dried whole.

Characteristics of dried product:
Leathery for short-term storage, hard for long-term storage.

Ways to use:
Dried mushrooms need not be rehydrated before adding to dishes where adequate liquid is present.

Rehydrate mushrooms before frying, spreading on pizza, or using as a side dish.

Marinate dried mushrooms in vinegar, oil, and spices before adding to salads.

Add dry to gravies, cream soups, egg dishes, stews, casseroles, and tomato dishes.

Rehydrate and add to rice dishes.

Mushroom Salad

1/3 cup olive oil
3 tablespoons red wine tarragon vinegar
1 tablespoon sugar
1/4 teaspoon dry mustard
1/4 teaspoon pepper
1/4 teaspoon salt
4 cloves garlic, minced
1 tablespoon dried parsley
1 small onion, diced
3 stalks celery, sliced
1/4 cup small dried bell pepper pieces
1 cup dried mushrooms
1 20-ounce can chick peas (garbanzo beans)
Lettuce leaves
Tomato wedges
Grated cheese

In a bowl combine olive oil, red wine tarragon vinegar, sugar, dry mustard, pepper, and salt. Stir. Add minced garlic, dried parsley, diced onion, sliced celery, and dried pepper pieces. Stir in dried mushrooms and drained chick peas. Cover and let sit for 3 hours. Serve on a bed of lettuce. Garnish with tomato wedges, and sprinkle with grated cheese.

Mushroom Soup

1 cup sliced or small whole dried mushrooms
1 10¾-ounce can chicken broth
1 cup chopped fresh onions
1/8 cup butter or margarine
2 cups water
1/2 teaspoon salt
1/4 teaspoon pepper
3 tablespoons flour
2 cups milk
2 dried bay leaves

Soak dried mushrooms in chicken broth in a large saucepan for 30 minutes. Drain mushrooms and return liquid to pan. Fry mushrooms and chopped onions in butter or margarine until onions become transparent. Return mushrooms and onions to chicken broth. Add water, salt, and pepper. Puree half the mixture in blender. Add flour and milk, and blend again. Return puree to remaining soup. Add bay leaves and bring to a boil. Reduce heat and simmer until thickened. Remove bay leaves before serving. Serves 4.

SUBSTITUTIONS

Dried onions can be used in place of the fresh onions. Decrease measurement to 1/2 cup dried onion, and rehydrate with the mushrooms. Add 1/2 cup additional milk.

OKRA

GENERAL INFORMATION

Water content of fresh food:
89%.

Selection of fresh food for drying:
Choose tender pods that are a minimum of 2 inches and a maximum of 5 inches long. Select pods that are free from blemishes.

Preparation for drying:
Wash pods. Remove stem and trim tips. Slice pods into ¼- to ½-inch pieces.

Characteristics of dried product:
Hard.

Ways to use:
Use in gumbos, soups, stews, and casseroles.

Grind into flour and use as a natural thickening agent.

Add to creole dishes.

RECIPE SUGGESTION

Okra and Rice

1 cup dried okra slices
1½ cups water
4 tablespoons butter or margarine
1/2 cup diced fresh onion
1 teaspoon dried garlic powder
1/2 teaspoon pepper
2 cups chopped fresh tomato
Cooked rice

Soak dried okra in water for 2 hours. Drain any remaining water. Place butter, onion, and okra in a frying pan. Add dried garlic powder and pepper. Stir fry until onion is transparent. Add tomato, cover, and cook until okra is tender. Serve over hot cooked rice. Serves 4.

SUBSTITUTION

Tomato leather pieces may be substituted for the chopped fresh tomato. Add a few tablespoons water to mixture before final cooking period.

ONIONS

GENERAL INFORMATION

Water content of fresh food:
88%.

Selection of fresh food for drying:
Both the bunching and bulb varieties dry very well. Harvest garden onions when the tops dry up, or sooner.

Preparation for drying:
Trim off top and root end. Remove outer paper shell. Cut into ¼-inch slices or dice.

Characteristics of dried product:
Leathery for short-term storage, brittle for long-term storage.

Ways to use:
Use dry to season soups, stews, and casseroles.

Rehydrate and add to salads.

Pulverize to make onion powder.

RECIPE SUGGESTION

French Onion Soup

1 cup dried onion pieces
1 10½-ounce can beef consommé
1/8 cup butter or margarine
1 tablespoon flour
1/2 teaspoon salt
1/2 teaspoon pepper
3 cups water
4 slices toasted bread
4 teaspoons Parmesan cheese
4 slices mozzarella or provolone cheese

In a large pan soak onions in beef consommé for 30 minutes. Gently cook over medium heat for a few minutes until onions are soft. Strain onions, reserving liquid in pan. Melt butter or margarine in a small frying pan, add onions, and fry until onions are transparent, approximately 2 to 3 minutes. Stir in flour, salt, and pepper. Return onion mixture to large pan and add water. Stir and heat through. Place toasted bread in four individual casseroles. Pour soup over bread. Top each with 1 teaspoon Parmesan cheese and a slice of mozzerella or provolone cheese. Bake in a 400° F. oven until cheese melts. Serves 4.

PARSNIPS

GENERAL INFORMATION

Water content of fresh food:
79%.

Selection of fresh food for drying:
Parsnips are long, fleshy, cream-colored root vegetables which resemble carrots. Harvest homegrown crops in late fall or early spring. Avoid soft or woody parsnips for drying.

Preparation for drying:
Wash. Cut off top stem and bottom end. Peel. Remove the core if woody. Cut into either ¼-inch slices, ¼- to ½-inch cubes, or ¼-inch strips.

Optional pretreatment:
Steam blanch small pieces 2 to 3 minutes, large pieces 5 to 7 minutes, or water boil 2 to 4 minutes.

Characteristics of dried product:
Hard.

Ways to use:
Dehydrated parsnips make zesty additions to soups or stews.

Rehydrate, cook, and serve as a side dish.

Add small pieces to sauces.

RECIPE SUGGESTIONS

Parsnip Patties

1 cup dried parsnip pieces
1½ cups water
1 lemon, juiced
Salt
1 tablespoon butter or margarine

In a medium saucepan soak dried parsnip pieces in water for 2 hours. Cover and steam until tender. Remove from heat and drain. Add lemon juice and salt to taste. Puree in blender. Form into four patties. Melt butter or margarine in a frying pan and fry patties until lightly browned. Serve as a side dish. Serves 4.

Fried Parsnips

1½-2 cups dried parsnip slices
Water
1/2 cup fine bread crumbs
Salt and pepper
2-4 tablespoons butter or oil

In a medium saucepan soak dried parsnips in water to cover for 2 hours. Cook over medium heat until soft. Drain and cool. Roll rehydrated parsnip pieces in bread crumbs, and season with salt and pepper. Fry in butter or oil until browned. Serves 4.

PEAS

GENERAL INFORMATION

Water content of fresh food:
78%.

Selection of fresh food for drying:
Pea pods should be well filled and snap easily. Peas should be sweet, tender, bright green, and plump, but not old.

Preparation for drying:
Shell.

Optional pretreatment:
Steam blanch 3 to 4 minutes, or water boil 1 to 2 minutes.

Characteristics of dried product:
Hard and wrinkled.

Ways to use:
Rehydrate, cook, flavor with dried mint, and serve as a side dish.

Add dry to soups, stews, and casseroles.

RECIPE SUGGESTIONS

Hamburger-Pea Casserole
1/3 cup dried garden peas
2/3 cup water
1 pound hamburger
4 large potatoes, peeled and sliced
1 tablespoon oil
1 teaspoon salt
1/2 teaspoon pepper
1 medium onion, diced
1 10¾-ounce can cream of mushroom soup

In a small saucepan soak peas in water for 1 hour. Cook over medium heat until peas swell and wrinkles begin to disappear. Add additional water during cooking if necessary. Meanwhile, brown hamburger, discarding fat. Parboil potatoes 5 minutes or until slightly translucent. Spread the oil evenly over the bottom of a large 9-by-13-inch baking dish. Drain peas and potatoes. Place half of the potatoes in the bottom of the baking dish. Season with half the salt and pepper. Layer onions, peas, then hamburger. Add remaining potatoes and seasonings, and top with cream of mushroom soup. Cover and bake in a 350° F. oven for 30 minutes. Remove cover and bake an additional 15 minutes. Serves 8.

Creamed Peas
1 cup dried peas
1½ cups water
1 tablespoon butter or margarine
1/4 cup chopped fresh onion
1 tablespoon flour
1/2 cup milk
1/4 teaspoon salt
1/8 teaspoon pepper

In a medium saucepan soak dehydrated peas in water for 1 hour. Simmer over medium heat until tender. Drain any remaining water. In a saucepan make a white sauce by melting butter and stirring in chopped onion. Cook until onion is transparent. Add flour. Cook gently over low heat for 2 to 3 minutes. Add milk and stir with a wire whip until thickened. Season with salt and pepper. Pour over cooked peas and serve hot. Serves 4.

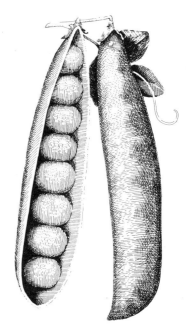

PEPPERS

BELL PEPPERS

GENERAL INFORMATION

Water content of fresh food:
93%.

Selection of fresh food for drying:
Select firm, thick-walled, fresh peppers. Green peppers ripen to red. Either may be successfully dried.

Preparation for drying:
Wash. Remove the stem and seed head. Slice into rings, strips, or ½-inch pieces. The seed core may also be dried.

Optional pretreatment:
Steam blanch 2 minutes, or water boil 1 minute.

Characteristics of dried product:
Crisp.

Ways to use:
Add to soups, stews, and casseroles without rehydration.

Rehydrate and add to salads or pizzas.

Pulverize and use as a seasoning.

Pepper seeds can be used as a seasoning in soups or stews.

RECIPE SUGGESTION

Vegetable Loaf (Pictured on page 44)
- 1/3 cup dried green pepper pieces
- 1/3 cup Spanish olive juice
- 3 tablespoons olive oil
- 1/2 cup diced Spanish olives
- 1 medium onion, diced
- 1 large or 2 small tomatoes, diced
- 1 loaf French bread

Soak dried green pepper pieces in olive juice for 2 to 3 hours. Add olive oil, diced Spanish olives, onion, and tomatoes. Stir. Cut French bread in half horizontally. Hollow out the inside of each half, leaving a shell approximately ¾-inch thick. Break the removed bread into ½-inch pieces and add to the vegetable mixture. Stir well. Stuff the French bread, place the stuffed halves together, and wrap in aluminum foil. Refrigerate 4 hours before slicing and serving. Serves 4 to 6.

SUBSTITUTION
If dehydrated onion is substituted for the fresh, add 1/4 cup additional olive juice.

HOT PEPPERS

GENERAL INFORMATION

Water content of fresh food:
93%.

Selection of fresh food for drying:
Jalapeno, chili, and banana are the most common varieties of hot pepper. If homegrown, harvest when peppers have reached maturity. Peppers should have firm, bright skins.

Preparation for drying:
Remove the stem and seeds. Slice into thin rings, strips, or ¼-inch pieces.

Optional pretreatment:
Steam blanch 2 minutes, or water boil 1 minute.

Characteristics of dried product:
Crisp.

Ways to use:
Use to season meats, stews, soups, or casseroles. Hot peppers are a strong seasoning and should be used sparingly.

Pulverize and add to Mexican dishes.

RECIPE SUGGESTION

Hot Pepper Jelly (Pictured on page 44)
- 1/3 cup coarsely pulverized dried hot peppers*
- 1/4 cup pulverized dried bell pepper
- 1 cup diced fresh onion
- 2 cups water
- 1½ cups white vinegar
- 1 1¾-ounce package Sure-Jell
- 1 6-ounce bottle Certo

*For color, texture, and flavor, a combination of Jalapeno, banana, and chili peppers is best.

In a large pot combine pulverized dried hot peppers, dried bell pepper, diced onion, water, and white vinegar. Let sit 15 minutes. Add Sure-Jell. Cook over high heat, stirring constantly, until mixture comes to a full rolling boil. Boil 1 minute. Remove from heat. Add Certo. Stir well. Skim off foam and stir. Pour into sterilized jars and seal. (Serve on crackers with cream cheese, or as an accompaniment to beef, pork, or meat loaf. Also good as an accent for oriental dishes.) Makes 9 cups.

POTATOES

GENERAL INFORMATION

Water content of fresh food:
80%.

Selection of fresh food for drying:
For best results, select grade A new or freshly harvested potatoes. Firm potatoes with a smooth, unsprouted peel and low starch yield the best dried product.

Preparation for drying:
Wash and peel. The green lining just under the skin must be removed or it will turn black. Cut away any bruised or damaged spots. Cut into ¼-inch slices, shoestring strips, or ½-inch cubes.

Pretreatment:
Steam blanch 5 to 8 minutes, or water boil 3 to 5 minutes. Potatoes may also be immersed in a mixture of 1/4 cup lemon juice and 3/4 cup water, sprinkled with lemon juice, or dipped in sodium bisulfite.

Characteristics of dried product:
Hard.

Ways to use:
Add to soups and stews.

Pulverize and use in pancakes.

Rehydrate, cook, and use in potato salad.

Pulverize and use for potato soup.

RECIPE SUGGESTIONS

Scalloped Potatoes
2 cups dried potato slices

1 13-ounce can evaporated milk

1 cup milk

1 10¾-ounce can cream of mushroom soup

1/2 cup dried mushrooms

1/2 cup diced fresh bell pepper

1 cup diced ham

1 cup grated cheese

Soak dried potato slices in evaporated milk for 1 hour. Drain potatoes, reserving liquid. Add milk and cream of mushroom soup to drained evaporated milk. In a large casserole dish that has been greased and dusted with flour, layer one-third of each ingredient in the following order: rehydrated potatoes, dried mushrooms, bell pepper, diced ham, cheese, mushroom soup-evaporated milk mixture. Repeat twice. Cover with aluminum foil and bake in a 350° F. oven for 1 hour. Remove aluminum foil and continue baking until top browns. Serves 4 to 6.

Party fare: Dill Deviled Eggs (page 110), Cucumber Dip (page 34), Vegetable Loaf (page 43), and Hot Pepper Jelly (page 43) with cream cheese on crackers

Fried Potatoes
2 cups dried potato slices

1½ cups water

3 tablespoons butter or margarine

Salt and pepper

Soak dried potato slices in water in a frying pan for 30 minutes. Cover the pan and steam until potato water evaporates. Add butter, and salt and pepper to taste. Fry over medium-high heat until crisp. Serves 4.

VARIATIONS
Add dried onion and dried bell pepper to potatoes while rehydrating. Fry in bacon grease and add small pieces of crisply fried bacon.

PUMPKIN

GENERAL INFORMATION

Water content of fresh food:
92%.

Selection of fresh food for drying:
Choose mature, rich, orange pumpkins with a firm, glossy rind.

Preparation for drying:
Wash. Cut in half and scrape away pulp and seeds. Remove rind. Cut into wedges 1 to 3 inches wide, then into strips ½-inch wide. Seeds can also be dried.

Optional pretreatment:
Steam blanch 3 to 4 minutes, or water boil 2 to 3 minutes.

Characteristics of dried product:
Hard.

Ways to use:
Pulverize and use to make pie or pudding.

Grind into a pumpkin meal and use in baking.

Dried seeds can be salted and eaten as a snack.

Pumpkin Leather
An alternative drying procedure.

- 1 6-8 pound pumpkin
- 1 13-ounce can evaporated milk
- 1/2 cup honey
- 2 teaspoons cinnamon
- 1 teaspoon nutmeg
- 1 teaspoon allspice
- Chopped dates, raisins, nuts, coconut (optional)

Cut fresh pumpkin in half and scrape out pulp and seeds. Cut into 2- to 3-inch slices. Place pumpkin, rind down, in ½ inch of water in a large baking pan. Cover and bake in a 350° F. oven for 45 minutes or until pumpkin is tender. Cool. Remove rind and mash pumpkin. In a large bowl combine 4 cups mashed pumpkin, evaporated milk, honey, cinnamon, nutmeg, and allspice. Place in blender and puree. Spread on leather trays, approximately 3/4 to 1 cup per leather sheet. Chopped dates, raisins, nuts, and/or finely shredded coconut may be added to the leather.

Pumpkin Seeds

- 1 teaspoon oil
- 1 cup dried pumpkin seeds
- 1/2 teaspoon salt

Heat oil in a small frying pan over low heat. Add dried pumpkin seeds and salt. Fry until lightly browned. Cool before storing.

RADISHES

GENERAL INFORMATION

Water content of fresh food:
95%.

Selection of fresh food for drying:
Any variety of radish can be dried. Harvest radishes when they are 1 to 1½ inches in diameter and before they turn woody, crack, or acquire dark spots. Fresh, firm radishes are best.

Preparation for drying:
Wash. Cut off top and root. Remove any damaged or darkened areas. Slice or dice.

Characteristics of dried product:
Leathery to hard.

Ways to use:
Rehydrate small pieces and add to salads.

Pulverize and sprinkle on salads or use in rice dishes.

Add to soups, stews, and casseroles as a seasoning.

Add small dry pieces to omelets.

Radish Sauce

- 1/3 cup dried radishes
- 1½ cups milk
- 3 tablespoons butter or margarine
- 2 tablespoons flour
- Salt and pepper

Place dried radishes in milk and let soak for 1 hour. In a saucepan melt the butter or margarine and add flour. Salt and pepper to taste. Stir. Add rehydrated radishes and milk. Simmer until tender. For a smoother sauce, puree in blender. (Serve over steamed cauliflower or other vegetables.)

SPINACH

GENERAL INFORMATION

Water content of fresh food:
91%.

Selection of fresh food for drying:
Choose fresh, crisp, tender spinach leaves.

Preparation for drying:
Remove any blemished areas. Dust or wash to remove sand and soil. For large leaves, fold lengthwise along the spine and cut out the vein with scissors.

Characteristics of dried product:
Brittle.

Ways to use:
Pulverize spinach leaves and use in salads.

Add small dry pieces to omelets, crepes, souffles, and quiches.

Crush and add to yogurt for salad dressing.

Pulverize and use to make cream soups and sauces.

Spinach Noodles

2 eggs
1/2 cup flour
1/2 teaspoon salt
1/2 cup dried spinach flakes
Flour

Beat eggs. Add 1/2 cup flour, salt, and dried spinach flakes. Mix well. Dough will be very thick and elastic. Roll out into a large square. Dough should be a maximum of ⅛-inch thick. Cut large square into fourths. Lay the pieces on top of each other and roll. Cut ½-inch pieces off the roll. Place additional flour on a cutting board. Separate the noodles and toss with flour to prevent noodles from sticking together. Spread noodles and let dry 1 hour before cooking. (To cook, boil in hot water for 15 minutes, or add dry to casseroles, stews, or soups.) Makes 2 cups raw noodles.

Cooked Spinach

1½ cups water
2 cups dried spinach
1 teaspoon salt
1/2 teaspoon pepper
Butter
Lemon juice

Bring water to a boil. Add dried spinach leaves, salt and pepper. Boil until leaves are soft, approximately 3 minutes. Season with butter and lemon juice. Serves 2.

SUBSTITUTIONS
Dried Swiss chard or beet tops can be prepared in the same manner. Lemon pepper can be substituted for the pepper.

SQUASH

WINTER

GENERAL INFORMATION

Water content of fresh food:
81%.

Selection of fresh food for drying:
Acorn, butternut, banana, and hubbard are only a few of many varieties of winter squash. Select mature squash with fully formed seeds and hard rinds. If harvesting, pick after the vines dry up. Squash should be heavy for its size.

Preparation for drying:
Wash. Cut in half and remove seeds and stringy fiber. Peel off rind. Cut into long strips about ¼-inch thick or into ¼- to ½-inch cubes. Seeds may also be dried.

Optional pretreatment:
Steam blanch 5 to 8 minutes, or water boil 3 to 5 minutes.

Characteristics of dried product:
Hard and brittle.

Ways to use:
Rehydrate, mash, and bake with cloves.

Rehydrate, mash, and use in dessert recipes.

Rehydrate and bake. Cover with provolone cheese during last few minutes of baking.

Toast and salt seeds, and eat as a snack.

Squash Pie

1½ cups dried squash pieces
1 cup water
1 cup evaporated milk
1/2 cup sugar
2 eggs
1/2 teaspoon cinnamon
1/4 teaspoon ginger
1/4 teaspoon powdered cloves
1/4 teaspoon salt
1 9-inch unbaked pie shell (page 27)
Cinnamon
Whipped cream

In a medium saucepan soak dried squash pieces in water for 30 minutes. Bring to a boil, turn off heat, and let sit until squash softens. Drain any remaining water and place squash in blender. Add evaporated milk, sugar, eggs, cinnamon, ginger, powdered cloves, and salt. Blend until smooth. Pour into unbaked pie shell. Sprinkle the top lightly with cinnamon. Bake in a 425° F. oven for 15 minutes, then reduce heat to 350° F. and bake an additional 30 minutes or until a knife inserted in the center comes out clean. Serve with whipped cream. Serves 6 to 8.

SUBSTITUTION
Pumpkin may be substituted for the squash.

SWISS CHARD

GENERAL INFORMATION

Water content of fresh food:
91%.

Selection of fresh food for drying:
Swiss chard is a large green leaf on a white stalk. Harvest when 8 to 10 inches in length and still young and tender.

Preparation for drying:
Dust or wash to remove debris. (Washing causes leaves to turn darker when dried.) Remove the spine by folding the leaf lengthwise along the spine and cutting out the vein with a pair of scissors. Stalks may also be dried. Cut into small cubes.

Characteristics of dried product:
Crushable.

Ways to use:
Use as a substitute for spinach.

Add dry to boiling water, cook, and serve with oil and lemon juice.

Pulverize and use in salad dressings or sprinkle on salads.

Pulverize and add to creamed soups for seasoning.

Pulverize the dried stalks and use as a thickening agent in soups, stews, etc.

RECIPE SUGGESTION

Swiss Chard Souffle

3 tablespoons butter or margarine
3 tablespoons flour
1 cup milk
1/2 teaspoon dry mustard
1/2 cup grated mild cheese
4 egg yolks
1/2 cup small dried Swiss chard pieces
4 egg whites

Melt butter or margarine in a large saucepan. Stir in flour and cook gently 2 to 3 minutes. Add milk and dry mustard. Cook over medium heat until thickened. Remove from heat and cool for 3 minutes. Stir in grated cheese. Add the egg yolks, one at a time, mixing well after each. Stir in the dried Swiss chard and set aside. Beat egg whites thoroughly but not stiff. Gently fold into batter. *Do not over blend.* Grease the bottom of a 1½-quart, straight-sided souffle dish and gently pour in souffle. Bake in a 350° F. oven for 35 to 40 minutes. Souffle should be high and golden brown.

SUBSTITUTIONS
Other light and thin dried vegetables may be substituted for the Swiss chard, such as mushroom slices, tomato slices, spinach, or vegetable leathers.

TOMATOES

GENERAL INFORMATION

Water content of fresh food:
94%.

Selection of fresh food for drying:
Choose firm tomatoes that have just turned red. Tomatoes that are too ripe will darken when dried. Green tomatoes can also be dried.

Preparation for drying:
Wash. Remove stem. Peeling is optional. (To peel tomatoes, immerse in boiling water for 15 seconds, then plunge into cold water. Skins should slip off easily.) Cut tomatoes into slices. Pieces should be uniform in thickness for even drying. For use as vegetable chips, sprinkle with lemon pepper or herbs before drying.

Characteristics of dried product:
Leathery for short-term storage, brittle for long-term storage.

Ways to use:
Dried green tomatoes may be used in relishes or chip dips.

Pulverize and make into paste or sauce.

Add dry to spaghetti sauces, soups, stews, casseroles, or eggs.

Pulverize and combine with other pulverized dried vegetables to make vegetable juice.

RECIPE SUGGESTIONS

Tomato Leather
An alternative drying procedure.

Tomatoes
Cornstarch
Herbs

Wash and core tomatoes. Place in blender and puree. For each 2 cups of puree, add 1 heaping tablespoon cornstarch. Cook over medium-high heat until tomatoes resemble the thickness of applesauce. Stir often. Remove from heat and allow to cool. Spread on leather trays, using 3/4 to 1 cup per leather sheet. Puree may be sprinkled with herbs before drying.

Tomato Leather—an easy and versatile alternative to home canning

Green Tomato Casserole

2 cups dried green tomato slices
2 cups water
3/4 cup bread crumbs
3 tablespoons melted butter or margarine
1 medium onion, diced
1 clove garlic, minced
1/8 teaspoon dried tarragon
1/2 cup grated cheese

In a medium saucepan soak dried green tomato slices in water for 4 hours. Cover and cook over medium heat until soft but not mushy. Drain, reserving liquid. Combine bread crumbs, melted butter or margarine, onion, garlic, and dried tarragon. Set aside. Lightly grease a 1½-quart casserole dish. Layer green tomatoes and bread crumb mixture, repeating until all ingredients are used. Add rehydration liquid. Sprinkle with grated cheese. Bake in a 350° F. oven for 40 minutes. Serves 6.

Green Tomato Mincemeat Pie

3/4 cup small dried green tomato pieces
1 cup small dried apple pieces
3/4 cup raisins
1 tablespoon powdered dried orange peel
1/4 teaspoon salt
3/4 teaspoon cinnamon
1/4 teaspoon nutmeg
1/4 teaspoon ground cloves
1¾ cups apple cider
3/4 cup buckwheat honey
1/8 pound suet
1 9-inch double-crust pie pastry (page 27)

In a saucepan combine the first ten ingredients and let sit for 1 hour. Add the suet which has been cut into very tiny pieces. Cook at a slow boil until mixture thickens. Pour into pie shell and cover with top pastry. Cut slits to allow steam to escape. Bake in a 450° F. oven for 10 minutes. Reduce heat and bake at 350° F. for 30 minutes.

SUBSTITUTIONS
Molasses or regular honey can be substituted for the buckwheat honey. Nuts may be added.

Pan-Style Pizza

1 pizza dough (recipe at right)
4 tomato leather rolls
1½ cups water
1/2-1 teaspoon dried oregano
1/2 teaspoon dried garlic powder
Toppings*
6 slices provolone or mozzarella cheese
1/4 cup Parmesan cheese

*Suggested toppings include cooked hamburger or sausage, pepperoni, bell pepper, black olives, onions, and mushrooms.

Let pizza dough rise in a large, greased cast-iron or oven-proof frying pan for 10 to 15 minutes. Place tomato leather rolls in water in a small saucepan. Add dried oregano and garlic powder. Cook until thickened. Spread sauce evenly over pizza dough. Add desired toppings and cover with slices of provolone or mozzarella cheese. Sprinkle with Parmesan cheese. Bake in a 450° F. oven for 20 to 25 minutes or until cheese melts and ingredients are cooked.

Pizza Dough

2 tablespoons dry yeast
1/2 cup warm water
5 cups hot tap water
12 cups whole wheat flour
2 tablespoons salt
2/3 cup oil
2/3 cup honey

Sprinkle yeast into the 1/2 cup warm water and let stand 10 to 15 minutes. In the Bosch Kitchen Machine or a large mixing bowl, combine hot tap water with 7 cups of the whole wheat flour. Mix until well blended. Add salt, oil, honey, and yeast mixture. Blend thoroughly. Slowly add small amounts of the remaining flour until dough begins to pull away from the sides of the bowl. Knead dough 10 minutes using the Bosch Kitchen Machine, or turn out onto a lightly greased surface and knead by hand for 15 minutes. Spread dough evenly in pan, and let rise as directed. Form remaining dough into small balls, corresponding to size of pizza pan, wrap and freeze for later use.

YAMS

OR SWEET POTATOES

GENERAL INFORMATION

Water content of fresh food:
74%.

Selection of fresh food for drying:
Choose firm, brown-skinned yams with orange flesh. Yams should have an unwrinkled skin and be free from bruises or decayed spots.

Preparation for drying:
Peel, wash, and cut into ½-inch slices or chunks, or coarsely grate.

Optional pretreatment:
Steam blanch 8 minutes, or water boil 5 minutes.

Characteristics of dried product:
Hard.

Ways to use:
Pulverize and use in dessert recipes.

Rehydrate, cook, and mash.

RECIPE SUGGESTION

Yam Tarts (Pictured on page 108)
1 cup dried yam slices or 3/4 cup dried yam pieces
2 cups apple cider
1/2 cup firmly packed brown sugar
1 tablespoon butter or margarine
1/4 cup granola
24 baked tart shells (recipe below)
Whipped cream

In a medium saucepan soak dried yams in apple cider for 1 hour. Place in blender and puree. Return to saucepan. Stir in brown sugar and cook over medium-high heat until thickened. Add butter or margarine and granola. Refrigerate overnight. Fill baked tarts with about 1 teaspoon filling. Top with whipped cream. Makes 24 tarts.

Tart Pastry
1/2 cup butter
1/2 cup sugar
1 egg
1½ cups flour
1/2 teaspoon vanilla

Cream butter and sugar. Add egg and beat well. Mix in flour and vanilla. Chill dough for several hours or overnight. Allow dough to soften before pressing into tart pans. Use thumb to press dough evenly. Place pans on a cookie sheet and bake in a 375° F. oven for 10 minutes or until golden brown. Cool, then remove from pans. Makes about 4 dozen.

ZUCCHINI
AND OTHER SUMMER SQUASH

GENERAL INFORMATION

Water content of fresh food:
94%.

Selection of fresh food for drying:
Zucchini can be harvested throughout its growing season. Unlike winter squash, immature zucchini is very desirable as the seeds are soft and the rind is tender. However, both small and large zucchini can be dried. Choose unblemished rinds.

Preparation for drying:
Wash thoroughly. Peel if desired. Cut into ¼- to ½-inch slices, chop into cubes, coarsely grate, or cut into julienne strips. If zucchini is larger than 12 inches, the large seeds and fibrous tissue should be removed. For vegetable chips, soak in barbecue sauce or soy sauce before drying.

Characteristics of dried product:
Crisp and hard.

Ways to use:
Dried zucchini chips can be eaten with dips.

Add dry to soups or stews.

Coarsely pulverize and use in dessert recipes and breads, or add to salads and salad dressings.

Add to tomato dishes.

Use small pieces in eggs and omelets.

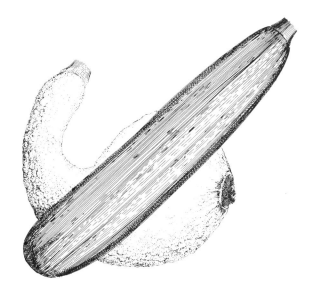

Zucchini Bread

1 cup pulverized dried zucchini

3/4 cup water

3 eggs

1 cup oil

2 cups sugar

2 teaspoons vanilla

3 cups flour

1 teaspoon salt

1/2 teaspoon baking soda

1 teaspoon cinnamon

1 cup chopped nuts

In a small bowl combine pulverized dried zucchini and water. Let sit 15 minutes. In a mixing bowl beat eggs and add oil and sugar. Stir in rehydrated zucchini and vanilla. Mix together flour, salt, baking soda, and cinnamon. Add to zucchini batter. Stir in chopped nuts. Pour into two medium-sized baking pans which have been greased and floured. Bake in a 325° F. oven for 1 hour or until a toothpick inserted in the center comes out clean.

Zucchini and Cheese Casserole

2 cups dried peeled zucchini slices

2½ cups water

1 medium onion, finely chopped

1-2 cloves garlic, minced

1/2 fresh green bell pepper, finely chopped

2 tablespoons olive oil

1 teaspoon dried basil

1/2 teaspoon salt

Pepper

6 sheets dried tomato leather or 12 ounces tomato paste

1/4 cup oil

2 eggs, beaten

1 cup bread crumbs

1½-2 pounds mozzerella cheese

1/4 cup Parmesan cheese

Soak dried zucchini in water for 1 hour. Drain, reserving rehydration water. In a large frying pan saute onion, garlic, and bell pepper in olive oil. Add dried basil, salt, and a dash of pepper. Stir fry until onion is transparent. Add dried tomato leather or tomato paste and rehydration liquid. Continue cooking until thickened. In another frying pan, heat 1/4 cup oil. Dip zucchini slices in beaten egg, then in bread crumbs. Fry until lightly browned on both sides. Grease a 1½-quart casserole dish and alternately layer zucchini slices, sauce, and mozzerella cheese. Repeat until all ingredients are used. Top with Parmesan cheese. Cover and bake in a 350° F. oven for 35 minutes. Uncover and bake an additional 10 minutes. Serves 6.

Dried zucchini makes into delectable Zucchini Bread

FRUITS

Dried fruits are the most popular of all dehydrated foods because of their exceptional flavor and versatility. After the water has been removed from fresh fruit, the high concentration of fruit sugar makes dried fruit much sweeter than fresh. It is a delicious and high-energy snack. Dieters find the chewy texture of dried fruit to be satisfying, reducing the desire to overeat. For cooking, dried fruit can be used in recipes in place of or in addition to raisins. Add dried fruit to breads, cereals, cookies, candies, ice cream, cakes, pies, cobblers, salads—the possibilities are limitless.

The Magic Aire II Food Dehydrator makes drying fruits beautifully simple. Most fresh fruits need only to be halved, cored or pitted, and sliced; the Magic Aire II does the rest. In selecting fruit for drying, choose produce that is attractive and at its nutritional peak. Drying will not diminish bruised areas or improve the flavor of underripe fruit. Overripe fruit may turn darker than normal.

Some fruits, such as apples, pears, peaches, apricots, and bananas, may darken when dried and when stored beyond 6 or 7 months. The Magic Aire II Food Dehydrator, however, with its unique heating and air-flow structure, dehydrates food in the shortest possible time, thus minimizing color change during drying and maximizing nutrition.

Preparation

Wash fruit in cold water and just prior to drying as water speeds up the deterioration process. Do not soak fruits because many vitamins and minerals are water soluable and easily lost by soaking. To prepare fruit for drying, remove stems. Pit or core the fruit, and halve or slice. Directions for preparing specific fruits for drying are listed on the following pages. Work quickly to get the fresh fruits onto the dehydrator trays in order to retain maximum nutritional value.

Dipping Pretreatment

If a color change is objectionable, fruit pieces may be dipped in a solution of lemon juice, orange juice, pineapple juice, ascorbic acid, or sodium bisulfite prior to dehydrating. The most natural dipping solutions are fresh or bottled lemon, orange, or pineapple juice. Use full strength or prepare with 2 parts juice to 1 part water. Crystalline ascorbic acid may be obtained from drug stores or in stores selling canning and freezing supplies. It is also an effective anti-oxidant. Mix 1 teaspoon ascorbic acid per quart of water. When using sodium bisulfite, use 2 teaspoons per gallon of water.

Prepare fruit as directed on the individual listing. Dip fruit pieces in the prepared solution or allow to soak for up to 5 minutes. Drain the fruit on paper towels before placing on the dehydrator trays.

Dipping is cosmetic for fruits that oxidize easily, but not necessary for the successful dehydration of fruit. Dipping and soaking increase drying time due to the additional water consumption. The Magic Aire II Food Dehydrator will successfully dry foods without pretreatment of any kind.

Sulfuring

Sulfuring is another method of preventing foods from darkening. It also shortens drying time and helps preserve the vitamin content. However, sulfur dioxide fumes caused by the sulfuring process can be very hazardous to your health. If you do sulfur fruits, dry them in the garage or in an extremely well-ventilated room.

Sulfuring is accomplished by placing fruit inside a sulfuring box and burning sulfur inside the box. A special sulfur box must be constructed of cardboard or wood, and approximately 1 tablespoon of sulfur burned per pound of food. The procedure is complicated, time-consuming, and not recommended. Foods can be pretreated in an easier and less harmful manner with dipping solutions.

The following books give detailed instruction on sulfuring and how to build a sulfur box: *How to Dry Foods*, Deanna DeLong, H. P. Books; *The Complete Book of Home Storage of Vegetables and Fruits*, Evelyn V. Loveday, Garden Way Publishing; *Putting Food By*, Janet Greene, Ruth Hertzberg, Beatrice Vaughn, Bantam Book.

Drying Time

The drying time for fruits ranges from 4 to 14 hours, depending on the thickness to which the food has been cut, the natural moisture content of the food, and the humidity in the air. Naturally the thicker the food pieces, the longer they will take to dry. Cutting fruit into uniform sizes helps to promote uniform drying. Drying time is also reduced by exposing more surface area. The faster the drying process, the better the color, flavor, and nutritional value of the dried fruit.

Check each individual fruit listing for characteristics of the dried product. Most dried fruits are leathery, chewy, pliable, and elastic. The fruit should not have any pockets or drops of moisture when cut with a knife. Remove fruit pieces from the Magic Aire II as they dry. For small pieces of fruits that may fall through the trays, the sprouting tray inserts or leather sheets can be used, or collect the small pieces at the base unit. Store dehydrated fruits in an airtight container. Label the containers, date, and place in a dark area.

Rehydration

Rehydration is the process of returning liquid to a dried food product. Fruits can be soaked in water, fruit juice, or appropriate liqueur. The flavor of dried fruit can also be enhanced by adding fresh or dried lemon, cinnamon, and whole cloves to the rehydration liquid. Fruits require from 1 to 2 hours to rehydrate, although some fruits may need to soak for as long as 8 hours.

The amount of liquid that fruits will absorb and the time necessary for rehydration varies according to the thickness of the fruit, the degree to which it has been dried, and the humidity in the air. As a general rule, to rehydrate dried fruit, soak in an equal amount of liquid. For example, soak 1 cup of dried apple pieces in 1 cup of apple cider. If the liquid is quickly absorbed, add additional liquid, a few tablespoons at a time, until the fruit will absorb no more. Rehydrated fruit should still be firm, not mushy. If liquid remains after rehydrating the fruit, use it for a fruit drink or for cooking the fruit.

Cooking

While dehydrated fruit does not necessarily need to be cooked, for some uses it is desirable to rehydrate to soften fruits. Dried fruit can be rehydrated and simmered in the rehydration liquid, or boiling water may be poured over the dried fruit which is then simmered in a pan for 10 to 15 minutes or until tender. Rehydrated fruits are sweeter than fresh fruits, but if sweetening is desired, sweeten to taste before cooking.

Dried Fruit Flakes and Powders

Fruit flakes are made by crushing hard fruit pieces between your hands or by placing them in a blender for a few seconds. Add fruit flakes to desserts, ice cream, jams, jellies, fruit salads, or fruit leathers. Label and store in an airtight container.

Fruit powders can be made by placing very dry pieces of fruit in a blender or mill and pulverizing them to a fine powder. Apples, bananas, rhubarb, blueberries, lemon peel, and orange peel are only a few of the fruits that can be made into a powder. Use fruit powders in desserts, breads, or fruit salads.

Powders also make excellent baby food by adding water, formula, or milk. Powdered dried fruits can be used as sweetening agents instead of sugar, honey, or maple syrup in baby foods. Remember that dried fruits are very concentrated in flavor.

Fruit Leathers

Fruit leathers are pureed fruits and fruit combinations which dry to thin sheets resembling supple leather. They are delicious and nutritious snacks which can be enjoyed by the whole family. Tasty, chewy, candylike leathers make great after-school treats, convenient desserts, fast-energy foods, and nutritious staples for the backpacker, fisherman, canoeist, or cross-country skier.

Fruit leathers are created by combining fruits, spices, flavorings, seeds and nuts; the amounts vary according to availability, taste, and imagination. Any fruit or combination of fruits can be used to make fruit leather. Apples, bananas, peaches, strawberries, pears, rhubarb, plums, apricots, cherries, nectarines, and papaya are all good choices for fruit leathers. Strawberry-banana, rhubarb-strawberry, cranberry-orange, pineapple-peach, carrot-orange, raspberry-apple, apricot-plum, banana-raspberry-coconut, and apple-orange-banana-sunflower seed are only a few of countless possible fruit combinations.

Leftover or overripe fruit, especially bananas, can be used very successfully for leathers. Damaged or decayed areas should be removed from the fruit before it is washed. Peeling is optional for peaches, apples, pears, and the like. Canned or frozen fruit may also be used. Cut fruit into chunks and puree in the blender. Most fruits are pureed in their raw state, but fruits such as apples or cranberries can be cooked to soften them. Strain cooked fruit through a sieve to obtain a smoother consistency, or puree in a blender. Add just enough fruit juice, applesauce, or water to the fruit to enable the blender blades to turn effectively. Pineapple juice, lemon juice, or ascorbic acid may be added to fruits that tend to darken. Remember, however, that the more liquid that is added, the longer the leather will take to dry.

Taste the puree to determine the flavorings that would most enhance the leather. Cinnamon, nutmeg, almond extract, vanilla, coriander, allspice, dried lemon peel, and dried orange peel make tasty additions to fruit leathers. Sweeten the puree with honey, maple syrup, or sugar, but remember that drying concentrates the natural sugars so leathers will taste sweeter after they are dehydrated. If the puree is good, the leather will be even better.

Finely chopped nuts, seeds, raisins, currants, figs, or coconut may be added to the puree, or they may be sprinkled over the puree immediately after it is spread on the leather sheets, half-way through the drying time, or before rolling up the dried leather. Because nuts and seeds contain oils which will turn rancid over a period of time, their addition will shorten the shelf life of fruit leathers.

Fresh fruit flavor preserved in fruit leathers

The Magic Aire II Food Dehydrator is easily adapted for drying fruit leathers with the fruit leather sheets. The thin plastic sheets are specially designed to allow for proper air circulation within the dehydrator. Place the sheets on the dehydrator trays, using only one half of each tray and alternating the halves. Sheets may also be covered with plastic wrap before spreading the puree. When the product is dry the plastic wrap easily slips off the leather sheet and can be rolled up with the leather for storing. To dry purees without the leather sheet inserts, cover one-half of each tray with plastic wrap, alternating halves in the stack.

For very thin or runny leathers, line one-half of the dehydrator tray with aluminum foil which has been turned up on the edges to form a tray. Place a piece of plastic wrap inside the foil tray before adding the thin fruit puree. Remove the foil as soon as the leather has dried sufficiently to hold its shape, and return the leather to the dehydrator tray for final drying.

Pour 3/4 to 1 cup of fruit puree on each leather sheet or plastic wrap. Puree should be about ¼-inch thick. Spread the puree evenly, leaving ¼-inch around the margins.

Dehydrate the leather until it can be easily peeled off the leather sheets or plastic wrap and until the center is no longer tacky. Most leathers dry in 8 to 10 hours, depending on the thickness of the leather, the water content of the food, and the amount of humidity in the air. The final product should be dry yet pliable. If the leather is difficult to remove from the sheet, use a knife to loosen and peel off the leather.

Roll the flat leather into a log shape. If desired, sprinkle with arrowroot or cornstarch before rolling to prevent the roll from sticking together. Roll two different kinds of fruit leathers together to make a delicious variation. For special treats, spread melted chocolate, caramel, carob, fudge, softened

cream cheese, or peanut butter on the leather before rolling. Banana-peanut butter, cherry-chocolate, and apple-caramel-coconut are delicious candy fruit leathers.

Fudge Filling

- 1 cup milk
- 2 cups sugar
- 2 heaping tablespoons cocoa or carob powder
- 2 tablespoons butter or margarine
- 1 teaspoon vanilla
- 10 fruit leather sheets

Combine milk and sugar in a heavy saucepan. Bring to a rapid boil. Add cocoa or carob and butter or margarine. Stirring constantly, cook until the fudge forms a hard ball when dropped into a cup of cold water. Remove mixture from heat. Add vanilla and stir until slightly thick. Before the appearance of the fudge changes from shiny to dull, spread on fruit leather sheets and roll.

Caramel Filling

- 2 cups brown sugar
- 1/2 cup molasses
- 3/4 milk
- 1/2 teaspoon salt
- 1/3 cup butter or margarine
- 1 teaspoon vanilla
- 12 fruit leather sheets

In a heavy saucepan mix brown sugar, molasses, milk, and salt. Bring to a boil, stirring constantly. Cook until the mixture forms a hard ball when dropped into a cup of cold water. Remove mixture from heat. Add butter or margarine and vanilla. Stir until caramel begins to thicken. Spread on fruit leather sheets and roll.

Store fruit leathers in an airtight container. Fruit leathers keep indefinitely when stored in the refrigerator or freezer. When kept at room temperature, leathers will store for approximately 6 months. If cream cheese is used as a filler, be sure to refrigerate the leather.

In addition to enjoying fruit leather as a delicious and fast-energy snack, leathers may also be used to make fruit soups, sauces, and beverages. For a fruit leather drink, puree 1 fruit leather with 1 cup of water. Let stand 15 minutes. Puree again. Place several ice cubes in a tall glass. Fill the glass half full with puree. Add gingerale or lemon-lime carbonated beverage. Stir. If needed, sweeten to taste with grenadine or sugar syrup.

Dried Fruit Equivalents

Use the Magic Aire II creatively to develop new specialties that are distinctively your own. When converting your recipes to dried fruit, you will generally need about 1/2 to 2/3 cup of dried fruit for each cup of fresh fruit. The following pages contain many recipes to help you begin using dried fruits.

MULTI-FRUIT RECIPES

Surprise Corn Bread Muffins

3/4 cup cornmeal

1/2 cup flour

4 teaspoons baking powder

1/2 teaspoon salt

1 cup milk

1 egg

1/4 cup melted butter or margarine

1/2 cup diced mixed dried fruit*

*Raspberries, plums, apples, pears, nectarines, pineapple, cantaloupe, or any combination of several dried fruits

In a mixing bowl combine cornmeal, flour, baking powder, and salt. Mix together milk and egg. Add melted butter or margarine. Add liquid to cornmeal mixture, stirring only enough to moisten. Fold in mixed dried fruit. Fill 12 greased muffin cups. Bake in a 425° F. oven 20 to 25 minutes or until lightly brown.

Fruit Yogurt

1 cup very small dried fruit pieces

1/2 cup water or apple cider

1 cup dry milk

4 cups water

1/2-1 teaspoon cinnamon

1 tablespoon honey

1 heaping tablespoon plain yogurt

Soak dried fruit pieces in water or apple cider for 30 minutes. Drain any liquid remaining after the soaking period. In a large saucepan mix dry milk, water, cinnamon, and honey. Heat to 110° F. Remove from heat and add the heaping tablespoon plain yogurt. Mix well, straining out any lumps. Place equal portions of the dried fruit in six yogurt jars. Pour in milk mixture, cover, and set in a culturing environment for 8 hours or overnight. Makes 6 8-ounce jars.

Gorp (Pictured on page 2)

2 cups raw sunflower seeds

1 cup roasted soybeans

1 cup chopped walnuts

1 cup raw cashew pieces

1 cup chopped Brazil nuts

1 cup raisins

1 cup chopped dried dates

1/2 cup chopped dried apricots

1/2 cup grated dried coconut

Combine all ingredients and store in an airtight container. Makes 9 cups.

VARIATIONS

Dried bananas, currants, other dried fruits, M & M candies, chocolate or carob chips may be added for variety. Almonds or filberts may be used.

Helen's Fruit Soup

1/2 cup prunes

1 cup seedless raisins

3 cups water

8 whole cloves

1 cinnamon stick

1 cup water

1/2 cup dried apricots

1/2 cup dried pears

1 cup water

3 heaping tablespoons tapioca

In a large pot combine prunes, seedless raisins, and 3 cups water. Simmer, without boiling, for 30 minutes. Stir gently. In a small pan combine the cloves, the cinnamon stick, broken into small pieces, and the 1 cup water. Cook 25 to 30 minutes. Place dried apricots and pears in small bowl. Add the remaining 1 cup water and let soak 30 minutes. Remove the cloves and cinnamon after simmering 30 minutes, and add the liquid to the prune mixture. Add rehydrated apricots and pears, plus any remaining liquid. Stir gently. Stir in tapioca. Bring to a slow boil and continue to stir and cook for 3 minutes. Serve hot or cold. Makes 5 cups.

SUBSTITUTIONS

Use cranberry juice instead of water to make a red fruit soup.

Sally's Fruit Salad

1/3 cup small dried papaya pieces

1/3 cup dried banana chips

1/3 cup dried pear pieces

1/2 cup coconut milk

2 fresh bananas

2 fresh apples

2 fresh tangerines

1 teaspoon crushed dried mint

2 teaspoons lemon juice

Lettuce leaves

Soak dried papaya pieces, banana chips, and pear pieces in coconut milk for 1 hour. Add fresh bananas, cut into ½-inch pieces; fresh apples, cut into ½-inch pieces; and fresh tangerines, sectioned. Toss with crushed dried mint and lemon juice. Serve on a bed of lettuce. Serves 2.

SUBSTITUTIONS

Apple juice or orange juice may be used in place of the coconut milk.

Granola with Dried Fruit

  4 cups rolled oats
  1/2 cup wheat germ
  1/2 cup bran
  1/2 cup sesame seeds
  1/2 cup coconut
  1/2 cup sunflower seeds
  1/2 cup cashews
  1/2 cup almonds
  1/3 cup oil
  1/3 cup honey
  1/2 cup chopped dates
  1/2 cup raisins
  1/2 cup chopped figs
  1/2 cup coarsely pulverized dried apples

In a large bowl combine rolled oats, wheat germ, bran, sesame seeds, and coconut. Coarsely grind sunflower seeds, cashews, and almonds. Add to mixture. Mix oil and honey in small bowl. Add to dry ingredients, a little at a time, until evenly mixed. Place mixture in a 9-by-13-inch baking dish. Bake in a 300° F. oven for 1 hour, stirring every 20 minutes, or dry on leather sheets in dehydrator. Add chopped dates, raisins, chopped figs, and dried apples. Cool to room temperature and store in an airtight container. Makes 10 cups.

SUBSTITUTIONS
Any type of dried fruit may be used in this recipe.

Mom's Oatmeal Fruit Bars

  2 cups packed dried fruit pieces
  2½ cups water
  1 cup orange juice
  2 tablespoons cornstarch
  1 cup sugar
  1 teaspoon vanilla
  1 teaspoon cinnamon
  1½ cups oatmeal
  2 cups whole wheat flour
  1 cup firmly packed brown sugar
  1/3 cup wheat germ
  3/4 cup butter or margarine, softened
  1/2 teaspoon salt

In a medium saucepan soak fruit pieces in water and orange juice for 1 hour. Add cornstarch, sugar, vanilla, and cinnamon. Cook over medium heat until thickened, stirring often. Cool. Combine the remaining ingredients. Place half of the oatmeal mixture in the bottom of a 9-by-13-inch pan. Spread cooled fruit mixture evenly over oatmeal. Sprinkle remaining oatmeal over fruit. Bake in a 325° F. oven for 45 minutes or until brown. Makes 24 bars.

APPLES

GENERAL INFORMATION

Water content of fresh food:
84%.

Selection of fresh food for drying:
Any variety of apple may be successfully dried. Tart apples become sweeter when dried. Select firm, mature apples with a glossy color and free from bruises and brown spots.

Preparation for drying:
Wash. Peel if desired. (Peelings tend to be tougher than the pulp. They may also be dried.) Trim away any damaged areas. Core and cut into ¼-inch slices, cubes, or rings. As a variation, dust with cinnamon before drying.

Characteristics of dried product:
Leathery and elastic for short-term storage, hard and crisp for long-term storage.

Ways to use:
Enjoy as a nutritious and delicious snack.

Rehydrate and add to cookies, pies, cobblers, and breads.

Add dry to breakfast cereals.

Pulverize and make applesauce.

Use pulverized peelings in teas, frostings, and dessert recipes.

RECIPE SUGGESTIONS

Fancy Apple Leather
An alternative drying procedure.

  5 cups diced fresh apples
  1/4 cup lemon juice
  1/2 cup cranberry juice
  4 tablespoons sugar
  1 tablespoon pulverized dried orange peel
  1/2 teaspoon cinnamon

In a medium saucepan combine ingredients and cook until apples are soft. Pour into blender and puree. Cool. Spread on leather trays and dry. Makes about 6 sheets.

Apple No-Cook Jam

  1 cup pulverized dried apples
  1½ cups apple cider or water
  1 teaspoon cinnamon

Combine pulverized dried apples and apple cider or water. Add cinnamon. Allow to rehydrate before serving. Keep refrigerated.

Caramel Apple Leather

1 14-ounce package caramels
5 sheets apple leather

Melt caramels in medium saucepan over low heat. Spread on apple leather sheets. Roll. Refrigerate until hard. Cut into ½-inch slices to serve.

VARIATION
Sprinkle caramel with finely chopped nuts before rolling.

Apple-Rice Pudding

1 cup very small dried apple pieces
1/2 cup apple cider or water
2 cups cooked brown or white rice
1/2 cup seedless raisins
2 eggs
1/4 cup honey
1/2 teaspoon salt
1/2 teaspoon vanilla
1/2 teaspoon coriander
2 cups milk
Nutmeg

Soak dried apple pieces in apple cider or water for 1 hour. Mix the cooked rice, seedless raisins, and rehydrated apples. Pour into a buttered 1½-quart baking dish. Beat the eggs until light. Add honey, salt, vanilla, and coriander. Stir well. Scald the milk and slowly add to the egg mixture. Pour over rice, raisins, and apples. Sprinkle top with nutmeg. Let pudding stand 30 minutes before baking. Set baking dish in a pan of hot water. Water should reach well up the side of the bowl. Bake 1 to 1¼ hours in a 350° F. oven. Serves 6 to 8.

SUBSTITUTIONS
Very small pieces of dried apricots, pears, or plums may be substituted for the apples. Finely chopped nuts may also be added.

Apple Spice Cookies

1 cup very small dried apple pieces
1/2 cup apple cider or water
1/2 cup shortening
1/2 cup firmly packed brown sugar
1 egg
1 cup dark molasses
1 teaspoon ground cloves
1 teaspoon cinnamon
1 teaspoon ginger
1/2 teaspoon baking soda
1/2 teaspoon salt
3 cups flour
Sally's Dried Apricot Bars Glaze (page 67)

Soak dried apple pieces in apple cider or water for 15 to 30 minutes. Cream together shortening and brown sugar. Add egg, molasses, rehydrated apples and any remaining rehydration liquid, ground cloves, cinnamon, and ginger. Mix well. Combine baking soda, salt, and flour. Gradually add to the creamed batter. Drop by teaspoonfuls onto ungreased cookie sheets. Bake 12 minutes in a 375° F. oven. Cool, then frost with Sally's Dried Apricot Bars Glaze. Makes about 5 dozen.

SUBSTITUTIONS
Small pieces of dried pears, plums, apricots, or fruit combinations may be substituted for the apples. Nuts or raisins may be added.

Apple-Rice Pudding, a delicious dessert

Apple Pie

3 cups dried apple slices
2 cups warm apple cider or hot water
1/2 teaspoon cinnamon
1/2 cup sugar
2 tablespoons flour or cornstarch
1/2 teaspoon cinnamon
Nutmeg
1 9-inch double-crust pie pastry (page 27)
1 tablespoon butter or margarine

Soak dried apple slices in warm apple cider or hot water for 30 minutes. Stir in 1/2 teaspoon cinnamon. Combine sugar, flour or cornstarch, remaining 1/2 teaspoon cinnamon, and a dash of nutmeg. Sprinkle half the mixture in the bottom of the unbaked pie pastry. Gently pour in rehydrated apples and liquid. Sprinkle with remaining sugar mixture. Dot with small pieces of the butter or margarine. Cover with top pastry and seal edges. Cut slits to allow steam to escape. Bake in a 425° F. oven for 40 minutes or until bubbly and lightly browned.

Apple Syrup

1-2 cups small dried apple pieces
1 lemon, juiced
2-3 teaspoons chia seeds
1-2 cups maple syrup

Loosely fill a 1-pint glass jar with small dried apple pieces. Add the lemon juice and chia seeds. Pour in enough maple syrup to cover the apples. Stir. Cover and let soak in refrigerator 3 to 4 days. (Serve over pancakes, ice cream, or fresh tofu.)

SUBSTITUTIONS
Sesame seeds or coriander seeds may be used in place of the chia seeds.

Christmas Jello

2/3 cup powdered dried red apples (dried with peels)
1 cup apple cider
1 3-ounce package lime gelatin
1 cup cold lemon-lime carbonated beverage
Whipped cream
Dried apple slices

In a medium saucepan combine the powdered dried red apples and apple cider. Let sit 10 minutes. Heat the applesauce just until it starts to boil. Sprinkle in lime gelatin, and when thoroughly mixed, remove from heat. Stir in cold lemon-lime carbonated beverage. Pour into mold and chill until firm. Decorate with whipped cream and dried apple slices. Serves 4.

Apple Brownies

3/4 cup small dried apple pieces
1/2 cup apple cider or water
1/2 cup butter or margarine
3/4 cup sugar
2 tablespoons cocoa
2 eggs, beaten
3/4 cup flour
1/4 teaspoon salt
1/2 teaspoon baking powder
1/2 teaspoon cinnamon
1/2 cup chopped walnuts
Brown sugar or powdered sugar

Soak dried apple pieces in apple cider or water for 30 minutes. Cream together butter or margarine, sugar, and cocoa. Add beaten eggs. Sift together flour, salt, baking powder, and cinnamon. Add dry ingredients to creamed mixture. Stir in rehydrated apples and rehydration liquid, plus chopped walnuts. Pour into a greased 9-by-13-inch pan. Bake in a 350° F. oven for 30 minutes or until done. Cool, then cut into squares. Sprinkle with brown sugar or powdered sugar. Makes 24 brownies.

Sour Cream Apple Pie

2 cups dried apple slices
3/4 cup apple cider or water
1/2 teaspoon cinnamon
2 tablespoons flour
1/4 teaspoon salt
3/4 cup sugar
1 egg, beaten
1/2 teaspoon vanilla
1 cup sour cream
1 9-inch unbaked pie shell (page 27)
TOPPING:
1/4 cup firmly packed brown sugar
1/4 cup white sugar
1/3 cup flour
1 teaspoon cinnamon
1/4 cup melted butter

Soak dried apple slices in water or apple cider and 1/2 teaspoon cinnamon for 30 minutes, stirring often. Drain and reserve 2 tablespoons of the apple liquid. Combine the flour, salt, and sugar. Add beaten egg and vanilla. Stir in sour cream, rehydrated apples, and the 2 tablespoons reserved apple liquid. Pour into unbaked pie shell and bake in a 400° F. oven for 15 minutes. Reduce heat to 350° and bake an additional 30 minutes. While the pie is baking, make the topping by combining the brown sugar, white sugar, flour, cinnamon, and melted butter. Mix well. Sprinkle topping on pie following the 30 minute baking period. Return pie to oven and bake an additional 10 minutes at 400°. Serves 6.

APRICOTS

GENERAL INFORMATION

Water content of fresh food:
85%.

Selection of fresh food for drying:
Choose firm, ripe apricots with good color. Avoid soft or damaged fruit. If homegrown, pick before apricots fall from the tree.

Preparation for drying:
Wash. Do not peel. Cut in half and remove pit. (The kernel in the center of the pit may also be dried.) Dry fruit pit-side up, or cut into ¼-inch pieces or strips.

Characteristics of dried product:
Leathery and pliable for short-term storage, hard for long-term storage.

Ways to use:
Dried apricots are nutritious fast-food snacks.

Chop and add to recipes as a raisin substitute.

Pulverize, rehydrate, and use as a sauce over ice cream.

Use in making preserves.

Add to cookies, pies, cobblers, and breads.

Use to make baby food.

Add to fruit salads.

Dried kernels can be used as a nut.

RECIPE SUGGESTIONS

Sally's Dried Apricot Bars (Pictured on page 76)
1 cup small dried apricot pieces
1/2 cup apricot nectar or water
1 teaspoon lemon juice
1/2 cup butter or margarine
2 cups firmly packed brown sugar
2 eggs, lightly beaten
1 teaspoon vanilla
1¾ cups flour
1 teaspoon baking powder
3/4 teaspoon salt

GLAZE:
2 tablespoons melted butter or margarine
2 teaspoons lemon juice
2 tablespoons apricot nectar
1 teaspoon powdered dried orange peel
1 cup powdered sugar
1/2 cup slivered almonds

Soak dried apricot pieces in apricot nectar or water and lemon juice for 15 minutes, stirring often. Cream together butter or margarine and brown sugar. Add lightly beaten eggs and vanilla. Sift together flour, baking powder, and salt. Add to creamed mixture. Stir in apricots and any remaining rehydration liquid. Pour into a greased 9-by-13-inch baking dish and bake in a 350° F. oven for 30 to 40 minutes. While bars are baking, make glaze by blending together melted butter or margarine, lemon juice, apricot nectar, dried orange peel, and powdered sugar. Mix until smooth. When bars are warm, not hot, evenly spread the glaze over the top. Sprinkle with slivered almonds. Cool completely, then cut. Makes 32 bars.

Apricot Jam
1½ cups coarsely diced dried apricots
1 cup water
3/4 cup honey
1/2 teaspoon powdered dried lemon peel
1/2 cup chopped walnuts or pecans (optional)

In a small saucepan combine apricots and water. Bring to a boil. Remove from heat, cover, and let stand 30 minutes. Add honey and powdered dried lemon peel. Bring to a second boil and boil gently, uncovered, over medium heat for 10 minutes or until jam is desired consistency. Stir in nuts. Pour into sterile jars and seal. Makes 2 cups.

Apricot-Banana Nut Bread
3/4 cup dried banana slices
1/2 cup lukewarm water
1/2 cup finely chopped dried apricots
1 cup sugar
2 tablespoons shortening
1 egg
3/4 cup milk
2½ cups flour
1/2 cup wheat germ
3½ teaspoons baking powder
1 teaspoon salt
3/4 cup coarsely chopped nuts

In a liquid measuring cup combine bananas and water. Let stand 1 hour. Stir to mash bananas. Add the apricots and enough water to make 1 cup. Stir again, and set aside. Combine sugar, shortening, and egg in a mixing bowl. Beat until smooth. Add milk. Mix together flour, wheat germ, baking powder, and salt. Add dry ingredients and rehydrated fruit to creamed mixture. Stir just enough to moisten. Add nuts. Pour into a greased 9-by-5-inch loaf pan. Bake in a 350° F. oven 60 to 70 minutes or until a toothpick inserted in the center comes out clean. Remove from pan and cool on rack. (For best flavor, wrap cooled bread in foil and let stand overnight before cutting.) Makes 1 loaf.

BANANAS

GENERAL INFORMATION

Water content of fresh food:
76%.

Selection of fresh food for drying:
Green, just ripe, or overripe bananas may all be successfully dried. The riper the bananas, the sweeter the dried product. However, overripe bananas will produce a darker dried product than green or just-ripe bananas.

Preparation for drying:
Remove skins and cut away bruised areas. Slice into ⅛- to ¼-inch slices or strips. Bananas may also be dipped in honey, sugar, or ascorbic acid to resemble commercially dried bananas.

Characteristics of dried product:
Leathery and slightly sticky in the center for short-term storage, crisp for long-term storage.

Ways to use:
Dried bananas are very sweet and make a wonderful candy substitute.

Pulverize and add to malts and blender drinks.

Add to breakfast cereals, cookies, breads, compotes, and jello.

Use to make baby food.

RECIPE SUGGESTIONS

Banana Leather
An alternative drying procedure.

   4 small fresh bananas
   1/4 cup lemon juice
   1/4 cup sesame seeds
   1/4 cup honey (optional)

Place the bananas, lemon juice, and sesame seeds in the blender and whip until smooth. Add the honey for a sweeter leather, if desired. Pour onto leather sheets and dry.

Banana-Nut Cookies

   1 cup small dried banana pieces
   2 tablespoons hot water
   3/4 cup butter or margarine
   1 cup firmly packed brown sugar
   1 egg
   2 tablespoons water
   1 teaspoon vanilla
   1½ cups flour
   1 teaspoon salt
   1/2 teaspoon baking soda
   1 cup chopped nuts

Combine bananas and 2 tablespoons hot water. Set aside. In a large mixing bowl, beat together until creamy the butter or margarine, brown sugar, egg, 2 tablespoons water, and vanilla. Stir together the flour, salt, and baking soda. Add to the creamed mixture and blend well. Stir in bananas and nuts. Drop by teaspoonfuls onto lightly greased baking sheets. Bake in a 350° F. oven for 15 to 18 minutes or until lightly browned. Makes about 5 dozen.

Banana-Carob Bars

   1 cup very small dried banana pieces
   1/2 cup milk
   1 teaspoon cinnamon
   1 cup flour
   1/2 teaspoon baking soda
   1/2 teaspoon baking powder
   1/4 cup melted butter or margarine
   1/2 cup honey
   1 egg, beaten
   1 cup bran
   1 cup carob chips
   1/2 cup raisins (optional)
   1/2 cup nuts (optional)
   Brown sugar (optional)

Place dried banana pieces and milk in a small bowl. Add cinnamon and let sit 15 minutes. In a large bowl sift together flour, baking soda, and baking powder. Stir in melted butter or margarine, honey, and beaten egg. Add the bran, carob chips, and rehydrated bananas and milk. If desired, stir in raisins and/or nuts. Pour into a greased and floured 9-by-13-inch pan and bake in a 350° F. oven for 30 to 35 minutes. After cake cools, sprinkle the top lightly with brown sugar, if desired.

SUBSTITUTIONS
Chocolate, peanut butter, or butterscotch chips may be substituted for the carob chips.

Banana Smoothie

   1/2 cup dried banana chips
   8 ounces yogurt
   8 ounces milk
   1/2 teaspoon cinnamon
   1/4 teaspoon vanilla
   Honey
   1-2 cups coarsely crushed ice

Place banana chips, yogurt, milk, cinnamon, and vanilla in blender. Whip until smooth. Add honey to taste, and blend again. Add ice and whip until ice is finely crushed and beverage is thinned to desired consistency. Makes about 3 cups.

SUBSTITUTIONS
Any dried fruits may be used instead of bananas. Combinations such as apple and cranberry are good. An egg may be added to make a nutritious breakfast drink.

Banana Smoothie made with wholesome yogurt and dried bananas

Banana Bread

1 cup pulverized dried bananas
1½ cups milk
1/2 teaspoon salt
1 teaspoon baking soda
1 teaspoon baking powder
1 cup whole wheat flour
1 cup white flour
1/2 cup oil
1/3 cup honey or 1/2 cup brown or white sugar
1 teaspoon dried lemon or orange rind
2 eggs, beaten
1 cup chopped walnuts
1/2 cup raisins (optional)

Combine pulverized dried bananas and milk. Let sit 10 minutes. Sift together salt, baking soda, baking powder, and whole wheat and white flours. Cream together oil, honey or sugar, and dried lemon or orange rind. Add beaten eggs and mix until smooth. Alternately add portions of the flour mixture and reconstituted bananas to the creamed batter, beating after each addition. Finally stir in the chopped walnuts and raisins. Pour into two medium-sized, greased loaf pans. Let batter sit in pans 10 minutes before baking. Bake in a 350° F. oven for 50 to 60 minutes or until a toothpick inserted in the center comes out clean. Cool before removing from pans.

BLUEBERRIES

GENERAL INFORMATION

Water content of fresh food:
83%.

Selection of fresh food for drying:
Blueberries should be fresh and ripe, yet firm. Overripe blueberries are soft and do not dry well.

Preparation for drying:
Remove stems and any leafy pieces. Wash if necessary. Shake trays to rotate the berries as they dry. To make a delicious candy, soak berries in honey for 2 hours before drying. (Blueberry leaves may also be dried.)

Optional pretreatment:
To break the waxy skins, pour boiling water over blueberries and let sit 2 minutes.

Characteristics of dried product:
Firm for short-term storage, hard for long-term storage.

Ways to use:
Pulverize and sprinkle on fruit salads and use in dessert recipes.

Rehydrate and use as a substitute for raisins.

Rehydrate and use in sauces, pies, cobblers, breads, and pancakes.

Add to breakfast cereals.

Use to make jams and jellies.

Make blueberry vinegar by combining 1 part dried blueberries and 2 parts white vinegar. Allow to stand 1 to 2 weeks.

Pulverize and add to baby cereals.

Use dried blueberry leaves in teas.

RECIPE SUGGESTIONS

Orange-Blueberry Leather
An alternative drying procedure.

1/2 cup fresh or frozen blueberries
2 tablespoons apricot or peach nectar
3 tablespoons honey
1 1-by-2-inch slice orange peel

Place all ingredients in a blender and puree. Spread on two leather sheets and dry.

Blueberry-Lemon Mousse

1/3 cup dried blueberries
1/3 cup water
1 teaspoon lemon juice
2 egg yolks
1/4 cup sugar
2½ tablespoons fresh lemon juice
1 teaspoon fresh grated lemon rind
1 egg white
1/4 cup whipping cream

Soak dried blueberries in water and 1 teaspoon lemon juice for at least 1 hour. Overnight soaking is best. Place egg yolks in the top of a double boiler. Beat until thick and pale, approximately 1 minute. Add sugar, 2½ tablespoons lemon juice, and grated lemon rind. Cook over boiling water, stirring constantly, until thickened, approximately 5 minutes. Let mixture cool to room temperature. Stiffly beat egg white. Whip cream. Fold the egg white into the egg-lemon mixture, then fold in whipped cream. Drain any remaining water from blueberries. Fold all but a few rehydrated berries into the mixture. Pour mousse into two stemmed glasses. Garnish with leftover berries. Chill thoroughly. Serves 2.

VARIATION
Mousse may be used as a filling for tarts (page 51) or pie (page 27).

Blueberry Pancakes

1 cup dried blueberries
1 cup grape juice
2 cups flour
3 teaspoons baking powder
1 teaspoon salt
2 cups milk
1/2 cup oil
1 tablespoon honey
3 eggs, beaten
Syrup

Soak blueberries in grape juice for at least 1 hour. Overnight soaking is best. In a small bowl sift together flour, baking powder, and salt. Place milk, oil, and honey in a large bowl. Mix well. Add beaten eggs. Add dry ingredients and stir just until large lumps disappear. Do not overmix. Form pancakes on a hot, greased griddle. Place 1 teaspoon rehydrated blueberries on top of each pancake. Turn pancakes when bubbles appear. Serve with hot syrup. Makes 24 pancakes.

Blueberry Muffins

1/2 cup dried blueberries
1/4 cup grape juice
1½ cups flour
1/2 cup sugar
2 teaspoons baking powder
1/2 teaspoon salt
1 egg
1/2 cup milk
1/4 cup oil

Soak dried blueberries in grape juice for at least 1 hour. Overnight soaking is best. In a large mixing bowl sift together flour, sugar, baking powder, and salt. In another bowl mix egg, milk, and oil. Add to flour mixture, stirring lightly. Do not overmix. Batter will be lumpy. Drain blueberries and add to batter. Bake in a 425° F. oven for 25 minutes or until muffins are golden brown. Makes 12 muffins.

CHERRIES

GENERAL INFORMATION

Water content of fresh food:
Sweet 80%, sour 84%.

Selection of fresh food for drying:
Both sweet and tart cherries can be successfully dried. The fresher the cherries, the better the dried product. Select firm yet plump, ripe cherries.

Preparation for drying:
Wash. Remove stems. Slice in half and remove pits. Dry pit-side up.

Characteristics of dried product:
Leathery and sticky for short-term storage, hard for long-term storage.

Ways to use:
Eat dried cherries as a snack.

Rehydrate in fruit juice and make into a sauce for ice cream.

Rehydrate and use in dessert recipes.

Use to make jams or jellies.

Add to fruitcakes, pies, cobblers, and ice cream.

Dip dried cherries in chocolate to make candy.

Pulverize and add to water to make a fruit drink.

Pulverize and add to baby food as a flavoring.

Pulverize hard dried cherries and sprinkle over desserts or fruit salads.

Use to make cherry vinegar (see Blueberries, Ways to Use).

RECIPE SUGGESTIONS

Cherry Pie

3/4 cup dried cherries
3/4 cup warm water
2 level tablespoons cornstarch
1/2 cup sugar
1 teaspoon lemon juice
1 cup water
1 9-inch double-crust pie pastry (page 27)
Flour

Soak dried cherries in 3/4 cup warm water for 30 minutes. Add cornstarch, sugar, lemon juice, and 1 cup water. Dust the unbaked pie pastry with flour. Pour in cherry filling. Cover pie with top pastry and cut slits to allow steam to escape. Bake in a 400° F. oven for 20 minutes. Reduce heat to 325° and bake an additional 20 to 25 minutes. Serves 6.

Cherry-Chocolate Cake

1/2 cup dried cherries
1½ cups water
1/2 cup shortening
1 cup sugar
3 heaping tablespoons cocoa
2 eggs
1 teaspoon almond extract or vanilla extract
2 cups flour
1½ teaspoons cream of tartar
1/2 teaspoon salt
1/4 cup milk
1 heaping tablespoon cornstarch
1 teaspoon baking soda

FROSTING:
1/3 cup milk
4 tablespoons mayonnaise
1 cup sugar
1 6-ounce package chocolate chips

In a medium saucepan soak dried cherries in water for 30 minutes. While cherries are rehydrating, in a large mixing bowl cream together shortening and sugar. Add cocoa. Add eggs, one at a time, beating vigorously after each addition. Add almond extract or vanilla. Sift together flour, cream of tartar, and salt. Alternately add flour mixture and milk to creamed mixture. Remove a tablespoon of the water from the rehydrated cherries and mix with the cornstarch. When no lumps remain, stir cornstarch into the rehydrated cherries and water. Cook over medium heat, stirring constantly, until mixture thickens. Remove from heat and add baking soda. Add cherries to cake batter. Pour into a well-greased and floured 9-by-13-inch pan. Bake in a 350° F. oven for 30 to 40 minutes. Cool cake. In a small pan heat milk, mayonnaise, and sugar to boiling. Boil 1 minute. Stir in chocolate chips and cook until chips melt. Spread on cooled cake.

CITRUS RINDS

GENERAL INFORMATION

Water content of fresh food:
Lemon, 90%; lime, 89%; Valencia orange, 87%; Florida orange, 73%; tangerine, 87%.

Selection of fresh food for drying:
Choose blemish-free, firm-skinned fruits which have been organically grown. Nonorganic citrus is generally sprayed with insecticides, and dyes are often injected into the rinds to improve appearance.

Preparation for drying:
Peel the fruit. Cut rind into ¼-inch cubes or small strips. (To dry the rind and fruit, do not peel. Cut into ¼-inch round slices and dip in sodium bisulfite or other dipping solution before drying. Otherwise, the fruit becomes very dark and unattractive when dried.)

Characteristics of dried product:
Hard.

Ways to use:
Use as a flavoring agent.

Use in hot teas or add to cold beverages.

Pulverize and add to frostings, breakfast cereals, or other desserts.

Add to sachets.

Make citrus peel vinegar (see Blueberries, Ways to Use).

Use whole slices of fruit and rind for garnishes on desserts, or float in beverages.

RECIPE SUGGESTIONS

Candied Orange Peel
An alternative drying procedure.

2 fresh oranges
1 tablespoon salt
Water
1 cup granulated sugar
1/4 cup water
1/2 cup powdered sugar

Thoroughly wash the oranges. Carefully peel, and cut peels into ¼- to ½-inch cubes. Place cubes in a covered container. Add salt and water to cover. Weight the peels down with a plate so they remain covered with salt water. Refrigerate overnight. The following day, drain and rinse peels. Place in a saucepan and cover with fresh cold water. Bring to a boil. Pour off water. Cover again with fresh water, and bring to a second boil. Drain, and repeat procedure one more time. Return drained peels to pan and add granulated sugar. Stir. Add 1/4 cup water. Cook until sugar mixture becomes translucent, approximately 5 minutes. Drain. (Sugar water may be saved and reused.) Sprinkle powdered sugar over peels. Stir. Place on sprouter trays in dehydrator, and dry until hard. (Use as a garnish, use in baking, or eat as a candy.)

SUBSTITUTIONS
Other citrus peels can be candied in the same manner.

Fruit Tea

1 dried orange rind, coarsely pulverized
1 dried lemon rind, coarsely pulverized
1 dried tangerine rind, coarsely pulverized
3 teaspoons crushed dried mint
2 teaspoons crushed dried rose hips
1 teaspoon cinnamon

Combine all ingredients and store in an airtight container. (To prepare tea, pour boiling water over tea, then strain.) Makes 16 cups of tea.

Lemon Pepper

1 tablespoon powdered dried lemon peel
1 tablespoon coarsely ground pepper

Combine powdered dried lemon peel and pepper. Store in an airtight container.

Lime Mustard

1/4 cup dry mustard
2/3 cup water
1½ tablespoons cornstarch
1/4 cup sugar
1/2 teaspoon salt
1/3 cup vinegar
1 teaspoon powdered dried lime rind
1 teaspoon orange juice

Mix dry mustard with 1/4 cup of the 2/3 cup water. Allow to stand. Mix the remaining water with the cornstarch, sugar, and salt. Add vinegar. Cook over low heat, stirring constantly until thickened. Remove from heat. Add powdered dried lime rind and orange juice. Cool. Stir in mustard mixture. Chill before serving. (Serve with lamb, chicken, shrimp, or egg roll.) Makes 1 cup.

SUBSTITUTIONS
Other citrus peels can be substituted for the lime peel.

Apple-Orange Frosting

8 ounces cream cheese
4 ounces butter or margarine
4 ounces plain yogurt
2 teaspoons vanilla
1 cup powdered sugar
1/2 teaspoon powdered dried orange peel
1/2 teaspoon powdered dried apple peel

Allow cream cheese and butter or margarine to soften to room temperature. Cream until well blended. Add yogurt, vanilla, and powdered sugar. Beat until smooth. Stir in powdered dried orange rind and powdered dried apple peel.

SUBSTITUTIONS
Lemon or tangerine peel may be used instead of the orange peel. Powdered pear peels may be substituted for the apple peel.

VARIATION
The powdered sugar may be eliminated, if desired.

COCONUT

Water content of fresh food:
51%.

Selection of fresh food for drying:
Choose fresh coconuts which are full of milk. Coconuts should be heavy for their size.

Preparation for drying:
Pierce the coconut and drain the milk. Split the shell and remove the meat. Coarsely grate or cut into ¼- to ½-inch cubes or strips.

Characteristics of dried product:
Hard.

Ways to use:
Use in baking instead of commercially dried coconut. Home-dried product will be slightly less sweet and more ivory in color.

Add to fruit salads and granola.

Eat as a snack.

Pulverize and use to sweeten baby food.

Sprinkle on fruit leathers before drying.

RECIPE SUGGESTION

Coconut Pudding

2-3 tablespoons flour or cornstarch

1 teaspoon pulverized dried orange peel

2 cups milk

2/3 cup honey or maple syrup

1/2 cup coconut

1/2 teaspoon vanilla (optional)

In a medium saucepan combine flour or cornstarch, pulverized dried orange peel, and milk. Stir in honey or maple syrup and coconut. Cook over medium heat until thickened. If additional flavor is desired, add vanilla. Serve warm or chilled. Makes 4 servings.

VARIATIONS

Small pieces of dried raspberries, strawberries, apricots, or banana may be added along with the coconut.

CRANBERRIES

GENERAL INFORMATION

Water content of fresh food:
88%.

Selection of fresh food for drying:
Choose fresh, dark red cranberries with shiny skins.

Preparation for drying:
Discard any imperfect cranberries. Remove any stems or leafy pieces. Cut in half. To dry whole, cover with boiling water for 1 to 3 minutes to break the skins.

Characteristics of dried product:
Hard.

Ways to use:
Rehydrate and make into relish.

Pulverize hard berries and use as a seasoning in breakfast cereals or dessert recipes.

Use to make preserves.

Pulverize and make into a beverage.

Use to make cranberry vinegar (see Blueberries, Ways to Use).

RECIPE SUGGESTIONS

Cranberry-Apple Beverage

1/2 cup dried cranberries

1 cup boiling water

1 cup warm apple cider

1/2 teaspoon cinnamon

Honey

Place dried cranberries in blender. Add boiling water and apple cider. Allow to soak 1 hour. Add cinnamon and puree until smooth. Add honey to taste. Strain if desired, and chill before serving. Makes 3 cups.

Cranberry Sauce

1 cup dried cranberries

1/2 fresh orange

2 cups water

1/4 cup honey

1/4 cup chopped walnuts

Place dried cranberries, 1/2 fresh orange from which the seeds have been removed, and water in a saucepan. Let soak 1 hour. Cook over medium heat until berries are soft. Add honey. Pour into blender and puree. Return mixture to pan and cook slowly until thickened, stirring often. Add chopped nuts. (Serve with poultry or as a topping for ice cream.) Makes 2 cups.

SUBSTITUTIONS
Raspberries or strawberries may be substituted for the cranberries and the sauce used as a dessert topping.

VARIATION
To make fruit leather, increase dried cranberries to 2 cups. Sweeten to taste with honey. Spread sauce on leather sheets, top with chopped walnuts, and dry.

CURRANTS

GENERAL INFORMATION

Water content of fresh food:
84%.

Selection of fresh food for drying:
Currants are small berries which dry to resemble raisins. Select currants which are ripe yet firm. All varieties can be dried.

Preparation for drying:
Remove stems and discard imperfect currants. Wash if necessary.

Optional pretreatment:
Cover with boiling water for 1 to 3 minutes to break skins.

Characteristics of dried product:
Leathery for short-term storage, hard for long-term storage.

Ways to use:
Use as a substitute for raisins. Currants are slightly more tart.

Use to make jams, jellies, and sauces.

RECIPE SUGGESTION

Currant and Rice Pilaf
1/4 cup dried currants
1/4 cup water
1½ cups uncooked white rice
1 teaspoon salt
1/2 teaspoon pepper
3½ cups boiling water
2 tablespoons butter or margarine
1/4 cup pine nuts

Heat currants and 1/4 cup water until currants swell and water is almost absorbed. Place white rice, salt, and pepper in an ungreased casserole dish. Add currants, rehydration liquid, 3½ cups boiling water, and butter or margarine. Mix well. Cover tightly and bake in a 350° F. oven for 45 minutes. Stir in pine nuts just before serving. Serves 6 to 8.

DATES

GENERAL INFORMATION

Water content of fresh food:
23%.

Selection of fresh food for drying:
Fresh dates grow in clusters on palm trees. Allow dates to ripen on the tree, and select before they become overripe.

Preparation for drying:
Wipe clean. Cut in half and pit. Dry halves, or cut into ¼-inch cubes.

Characteristics of dried product:
Soft for short-term storage, leathery and chewy for long-term storage.

Ways to use:
Use in breads, muffins, candies, and desserts.

Add to breakfast cereals and trail mixes.

Pulverize hard dates and use as a sweetener.

Pulverize and sprinkle on puddings.

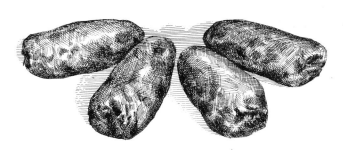

Date Balls

    1 pound dried dates (about 48)
    1/2 cup peanut butter
    1/2 cup granola or 1/2-1 cup toasted oats
    1 cup coconut

Cut dates into small pieces. Mix together with peanut butter, granola or toasted oats, and 1/2 cup coconut. Form into small balls 1 inch in diameter. Roll in remaining 1/2 cup coconut. Makes 24 to 36 balls.

VARIATION

Sesame seeds, sunflower seeds, carob chips, or peanut butter chips may be added for variety. Chopped figs may be substituted for the dates.

FIGS

GENERAL INFORMATION

Water content of fresh food:
  78%.

Selection of fresh food for drying:
  Pick when fully ripe and soft. Figs can also be harvested just as they fall from the tree.

Preparation for drying:
  Check for mold or decay. Cut in half or into small pieces. The thin skin does not need to be peeled.

Characteristics of dried product:
  Sticky for short-term storage, leathery for long-term storage.

Ways to use:
  Enjoy as a sweet and delicious snack.

  Add to desserts, cakes, cookies, breads, breakfast foods, and puddings.

  Use to make a filling for baked products.

  Pulverize and add to baby cereal.

RECIPE SUGGESTION

Fig-Filled Cookies (Pictured on page 108)

    FIG FILLING:
    2½ cups chopped dried figs
    1/2 cup hot water
    1/4 cup honey
    1 tablespoon butter or margarine

    COOKIE DOUGH:
    4 cups flour
    1 teaspoon baking soda
    1 teaspoon baking powder
    1 teaspoon salt
    1½ cups sugar
    1 cup shortening
    1/2 cup sour cream
    1 teaspoon vanilla
    2 eggs
    2 egg whites, slightly beaten (optional)

Prepare the filling by combining the figs, hot water, honey, and butter or margarine. Cook over low heat until figs are soft. Remove from heat and mash slightly. To prepare the dough, stir together flour, baking soda, baking powder, and salt. In a large bowl blend sugar, shortening, sour cream, vanilla, and eggs. On a floured board, roll out dough ⅛- to ¼-inch thick. Cut into circles using a 2-inch cutter, and place on a lightly greased cookie sheet. Put 1 teaspoon of fig filling in the center of each circle. Place another circle on top of the filling. Seal the edges with the fingers or the tines of a fork. Brush with beaten egg whites, if desired. Bake in a 375° F. oven for 12 to 15 minutes. Makes 4 dozen.

SUBSTITUTIONS

Dates, raisins, apricots, cherries, or other dried fruits may be used in place of the figs.

GRAPES/RAISINS

GENERAL INFORMATION

Water content of fresh food:
  82%.

Selection of fresh food for drying:
  Seedless varieties are the easiest to dry, but grapes with seeds can be successfully dried if the seeds are removed. Select grapes that are plump, firm, and ripe. Wild grapes may also be dried.

Preparation for drying:
  Remove stems and discard imperfect grapes. Wash if needed. If cut in half, place cut side up on the tray.

Optional pretreatment:
  To dry whole grapes, cover with boiling water for 1 to 3 minutes to break the skins.

Characteristics of dry product:
  Sticky for short-term storage, raisinlike for long-term storage.

Ways to use:
  Use in baking.

  Add to salads, stuffings, and hot cereals.

  Pulverize and make into a fruit drink.

For afternoon tea: Date Balls, Sally's Dried Apricot Bars (page 67), and Apple-Mint Tea (page 113)

Frosted Grapes

An alternative drying procedure.

Fresh grapes
1 egg white
Granulated sugar

Cut grapes in half. Remove seeds if necessary. Beat egg white until frothy, but not stiff. Dip grapes in egg white, then roll in granulated sugar. Place on dehydrator trays, and dry until brittle.

Apple and Raisin Cookies

1 cup dried apple pieces
4 tablespoons hot water
3/4 cup butter or margarine
1 cup firmly packed brown sugar
1 egg
2 tablespoons water
1 teaspoon vanilla
1 cup flour
1 teaspoon salt
1/2 teaspoon baking soda
3 cups granola
2/3 cup raisins

Combine dried apple pieces and 4 tablespoons hot water. Set aside. In a large bowl beat together until creamy the butter or margarine, brown sugar, egg, 2 tablespoons water, and vanilla. Stir together flour, salt, and baking soda. Add to creamed mixture and blend. Stir in apples and any remaining rehydration liquid, granola, and raisins. Drop by teaspoonfuls onto lightly greased baking sheet. Bake in a 350° F. oven for 15 to 18 minutes or until lightly browned. Makes 5 dozen.

Raisin Bread

1 cup milk
2 tablespoons butter or margarine
3 tablespoons firmly packed brown sugar
3/4 teaspoon salt
3/4 teaspoon cinnamon
1 package dry yeast
1/4 cup lukewarm water
1 teaspoon sugar
2½ cups white flour
1 cup raisins
1 cup whole wheat flour
Apple-Orange Frosting (optional) (page 73)

Scald milk. Add butter or margarine, brown sugar, salt, and cinnamon. Stir. Cool to lukewarm. Dissolve dry yeast in lukewarm water. Add sugar and let stand 10 minutes. Mix dissolved yeast with milk mixture. Stir in white flour and raisins. Mix well. Add whole wheat flour. Knead 10 minutes with the Bosch Kitchen Machine or turn out on a lightly floured board and hand knead until smooth and satiny. Place in a greased bowl and cover. Let rise until double in bulk. Place in one large or two small greased loaf pans. Cover and let rise again until nearly double in bulk. Bake in a 400° F. oven for 15 minutes. Reduce heat to 375° F. and bake for an additional 25 minutes. Glaze with Apple-Orange Frosting, if desired.

SUBSTITUTIONS

Dried cherries may be substituted for the raisins.

MELONS

Water content of fresh food:

Cantaloupe, 91%; casaba, 92%; honeydew, 91%; watermelon, 92%.

Selection of fresh food for drying:

Choose ripe but not overripe melons which are fragrant and heavy. Cantaloupe, casaba, and honeydew should yield slightly to pressure. Cantaloupe seams should not be too green. Watermelon should sound hollow when thumped.

Preparation for drying:

Cut in half. Discard any seeds or stringy pulp. Slice into wedges and trim off rind. Melons are primarily water, therefore cut into ¾- to 1-inch pieces to dry. If the fresh fruit is sliced too thinly, the dried product cannot be easily removed from the dehydrator trays.

Characteristics of dried product:

Leathery.

Ways to use:

Enjoy as a snack.

Add small pieces to fruit salad.

Rehydrate and make into a sauce for ice cream.

Add small pieces to cookies and cakes.

Add to fruit cups.

Candy Melon

An alternative drying procedure.

1 melon
3/4 cup powdered sugar
1 tablespoon ginger

Halve the melon and remove the seeds. Cut away rind, and cut into 1-inch cubes. Mix together powdered sugar and ginger. Dip one side of each melon piece into the ginger mixture. Place dipped side up on the drying trays. Dry until hard.

Crunchy Cantaloupe Leather

An alternative drying procedure.

1 cup diced fresh cantaloupe
1/3 cup applesauce
Cinnamon
2 tablespoons flaked coconut
3 tablespoons slivered almonds

Puree cantaloupe. Add applesauce. Season to taste with cinnamon. Pour onto two leather sheets. Sprinkle with coconut and slivered almonds and dry.

Honeydew Fruit Soup

1 cup dried honeydew melon
2 cups chicken broth
1/4 teaspoon ginger
1/4 teaspoon cinnamon
2 tablespoons butter
1 tablespoon firmly packed brown sugar
1 cup light cream
1 cup milk
1/4 cup diced ham or prosciutto
Crushed dried mint

In a medium saucepan combine dried honeydew melon and chicken broth. Let stand 1 hour. Add ginger, cinnamon, butter, and brown sugar. Cook until melon softens. Place in a blender and puree. Add light cream and milk. Stir. Refrigerate until cold. Garnish with diced ham or prosciutto and crushed dried mint, and serve as an appetizer soup. Serves 4 to 6.

Watermelon Sherbet

1 cup dried watermelon pieces
2 cups water
1½ cups sugar
1/2 cup frozen orange juice concentrate
2 egg whites

In a saucepan cook dried watermelon pieces in water until soft, approximately 15 minutes. Stir often. Place in blender and puree. Add water if necessary until puree measures 2 cups. Return to pan, add sugar, and stir over low heat until sugar is dissolved. Stir in orange juice concentrate. Transfer to a bowl and freeze until firm. When frozen, add unbeaten egg whites. Beat until mixture is fluffy and lighter in color. Return to freezer and freeze until firm. Serves 6.

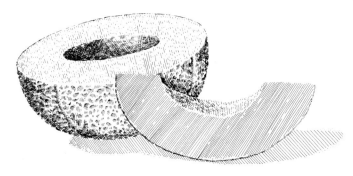

Cantaloupe Custard Pie

4 eggs
1/2 cup sugar
1/4 teaspoon salt
3 cups hot milk
Nutmeg
1/4 cup pulverized dried cantaloupe
2 9-inch unbaked pie shells (page 27)

TOPPING:
2 tablespoons dried orange peel
1 cup raw sunflower seeds
2 tablespoons coconut
1/2 teaspoon cinnamon

In a large bowl combine eggs, sugar, and salt. Beat with electric mixer until light peaks form. Stir in hot milk, a dash nutmeg, and pulverized dried cantaloupe. Pour into unbaked pie shells. Bake in a 450° F. oven for 10 minutes. Reduce heat to 350° and bake an additional 35 to 40 minutes or until a knife inserted in the center comes out clean. Cool. To prepare topping, pulverize dried orange peel to a fine powder. Remove from blender and pulverize the sunflower seeds. Combine powdered orange peel, pulverized sunflower seeds, coconut, and cinnamon. Sprinkle over pies. Serves 12.

NECTARINES

GENERAL INFORMATION

Water content of fresh food:
82%.

Selection of fresh food for drying:
The nectarine has a smoother skin, brighter color, and richer flavor than the peach. Select fresh, firm nectarines with tender skins.

Preparation for drying:
Wash. Cut in half and remove pit. Peeling is optional. Cut into ¼- to ½-inch slices or ½- to ¾-inch cubes.

Characteristics of dried product:
Leathery for short-term storage, firm for long-term storage.

Ways to use:
Eat as a snack.

Add to dessert recipes, fruit salads, and breakfast cereals.

Reconstitute and use for pies and cobblers.

Add to muffins and pancakes.

Make into syrup.

Pulverize and use for baby food.

Nectarine Angel Cake

1 packaged angel food cake

2 cups dried nectarine slices

2 cups water or fruit juice

1 teaspoon cinnamon

1/4 cup sugar

2 tablespoons apricot nectar or orange juice

1 cup whipping cream

1 teaspoon vanilla

1 teaspoon sugar

Prepare angel food cake according to package directions. In a saucepan soak dried nectarine slices in water or fruit juice for 1 hour. Add cinnamon, and bring to a boil. Cook until most of the liquid has been absorbed, approximately 10 minutes. Stir often. Place fruit in a blender and puree. Add 1/4 cup sugar and apricot nectar or orange juice. Mix well. Chill. In a small bowl whip the whipping cream until soft peaks form, and flavor with vanilla and 1 teaspoon sugar. Gently fold the chilled nectarine puree into the whipped cream. Slice the angel food cake into four horizontal layers. Spread the filling between each layer, and chill before serving.

PAPAYA

GENERAL INFORMATION

Water content of fresh food:
89%.

Selection of fresh food for drying:
Select papayas that are soft and ripe, but not mushy. The green skin of the papaya turns yellow when the fruit is ripe.

Preparation for drying:
Cut the papaya in half and remove the black seeds. Peel. Cut into ¼- to ½-inch strips or chunks.

Characteristics of dried product.
Leathery for short-term storage, brittle for long-term storage.

Ways to use:
Eat dried as a delicious snack.

Rehydrate and add to cookies, cakes, muffins, and breakfast cereals.

Pulverize and use to flavor and tenderize meat.

Pulverize and add to baby food.

Pulverize and use flakes to flavor salads and dessert recipes.

Papaya Sauce

2/3 cup small dried papaya pieces or 1/3 cup pulverized dried papaya

1 teaspoon powdered dried orange peel

1½ cups water

1 cup small or 12 large marshmallows, cut up

Place small papaya pieces or pulverized papaya, dried orange peel, and water in a small saucepan. Rehydrate for 15 minutes, then cook until papaya is soft. Add marshmallows and stir until melted. (Serve warm over plain yogurt, tofu, or ice cream. Top with grated coconut, if desired.) Makes 1 cup.

PEACHES

GENERAL INFORMATION

Water content of fresh food:
89%.

Selection of fresh food for drying:
Choose ripe but firm peaches without bruised or spoiled spots. All varieties dry well. Both freestone and clingstone dehydrate successfully. The riper the peach, the sweeter the dried product. However, overripe peaches turn dark when dried.

Preparation for drying:
Wash. Cut in half and remove stone. Peel if desired. Cut into ¼- to ½-inch slices or ½- to ¾-inch cubes.

Characteristics of dried product:
Chewy for short-term storage, brittle for long-term storage.

Ways to use:
Rehydrate and add to pies, cobblers, ice cream, breakfast foods, and compotes.

Enjoy dry as a tasty and healthy treat.

Use to make jams and jellies.

Pulverize and use to make baby food.

Pulverize and sprinkle on fruit salads.

Fresh Peach Jam
An alternative drying procedure.

7 cups peeled and sliced fresh peaches

4 tablespoons lemon juice

1/2-1 cup honey

Puree peaches and lemon juice in blender. Add honey to taste. Spread mixture ⅜-inch thick on leather sheets. Place in dehydrator and dry 3 to 3½ hours. Stir and re-spread jam about once each hour. When mixture is the consistency of jam, pour into a glass jar and refrigerate or freeze. Makes 1 cup.

SUBSTITUTIONS

Almost any fruit or berry can be substituted for the peaches.

Peach Ice Cream
2 cups dried peaches

2 cups lukewarm water

3/4 cup sugar

1/3 cup water

1/4 teaspoon cinnamon

2 tablespoons light corn syrup

2 egg whites

1/2 cup whipping cream

Combine peaches and 2 cups lukewarm water. Let stand 1 hour, stirring occasionally. Pour into blender and puree until smooth. Set aside. Combine sugar, 1/3 cup water, cinnamon, and corn syrup in a saucepan. Cook over medium heat, stirring constantly, until sugar is dissolved, then bring to a boil without stirring. Boil until mixture reaches soft-ball stage—234° to 240° on a candy thermometer or until a small amount spooned into ice water can be molded into a soft ball. Meanwhile, beat egg whites until stiff but not dry. In a separate bowl beat whipping cream until soft peaks form. When sugar mixture reaches the soft-ball state, remove from heat immediately. Slowly pour into egg whites, beating constantly on high speed of electric mixer. Continue beating until mixture is thick and shiny. Fold peach puree into whipped cream. Gradually pour peach mixture into egg whites, beating slowly to blend. Pour into a loaf pan or 1½-quart container. Cover with plastic wrap and freeze. Ice cream may also be frozen in a churn-type freezer.

Breakfast Peaches
2 cups small dried peach pieces

1 cup water

2 tablespoons honey

1 cup granola

2 tablespoons butter or margarine

Milk

Place dried peaches, water, and honey in an 8- or 9-inch square glass pan. Sprinkle granola over peaches. Dot with butter or margarine. Bake in a 350° F. oven for 30 to 40 minutes. Serve warm with milk. Serves 4.

SUBSTITUTIONS

Pears, apples, apricots, or nectarines may be used instead of peaches.

PEARS

GENERAL INFORMATION

Water content of fresh food:
83%.

Selection of fresh food for drying:
Choose any good eating variety. Pick pears from the tree while they are still green, and allow pears to ripen before drying. Pears should be firm to the touch, yet ripe.

Preparation for drying:
Wash. Peel if desired. (Peelings become more tart and grainy than the white flesh.) Remove the stem and cut out the woody vein and core. Cut into ¼- to ½-inch strips or cubes.

Characteristics of dried products:
Leathery for short-term storage, brittle for long-term storage.

Ways to use:
Eat dried pears as a nutritious snack.

Rehydrate and use in fruit sauces.

Add to cereals, breakfast foods, breads, and desserts.

Use to make baby food.

Pulverize peels and use as a flavoring in fruit salads, breads, and cobblers.

RECIPE SUGGESTIONS

Tutti-Fruit
An alternative drying procedure.

1 3-ounce package gelatin, any flavor

1 cup boiling water

1 cup cold water

Fresh pears, peeled and sliced

Dissolve gelatin in boiling water, then add cold water. Soak pear slices in gelatin water for 10 minutes. Blot dry on paper towels. Dehydrate until dry.

Pear Bread (Pictured on page 108)

1 cup small dried pear pieces

1 cup water

3 tablespoons soft butter or margarine

1 cup sugar

1 egg

1/2 cup orange juice

2 cups flour

2 teaspoons baking powder

1/2 teaspoon baking soda

3/4 teaspoon salt

1/2 cup chopped nuts

GLAZE:

2 tablespoons melted butter or margarine

2 tablespoons lemon juice

2 tablespoons apricot nectar

1 teaspoon powdered dried orange peel

1 cup powdered sugar

Soak dried pear pieces in water for 30 minutes. Drain, saving 1/4 cup of the rehydration water. Set aside. Cream butter or margarine, sugar, and egg. Add orange juice and 1/4 cup rehydration water. In a separate bowl mix flour, baking powder, baking soda, and salt. Gradually add the creamed mixture. Stir in rehydrated pears and chopped nuts. Pour into one greased 9-by-5-inch pan or three 2-by-5-inch pans. Bake in a 350° F. oven for 35 to 45 minutes, depending on pan size, or until a toothpick comes out clean. Cool 10 minutes before removing from pan. Make glaze by blending together melted butter or margarine, lemon juice, apricot nectar, dried orange peel, and powdered sugar. Spread evenly over slightly warm loaves.

PINEAPPLE

GENERAL INFORMATION

Water content of fresh food:
85%.

Selection of fresh food for drying:
Choose firm pineapples with a rich golden color and a sweet smell. Pineapples are ripe when a leaf can be easily plucked from the crown.

Preparation for drying:
Remove crown and cut away skin and eyes. For rings, cut into ¼- to ½-inch slices, then cut out core. For pieces, halve the pineapple, remove core, and cut into ¼-inch pieces. Canned pineapple which has been packed in its own juice can be dried to make a delicious candy. Save pineapple juice drippings to dip other fruits in to prevent darkening during drying.

Characteristics of dried products:
Leathery for short-term storage, hard for long-term storage.

Ways to use:
Enjoy as a nutritious dried fruit treat.

Add to dessert recipes, candies, and fruit salads.

Pulverize and add to baby foods to sweeten.

Pulverize and sprinkle over fruit salads and ham.

Make pineapple vinegar (see Blueberries, Ways to Use).

RECIPE SUGGESTIONS

Pineapple-Poppy Seed Cake

1/2 cup powdered dried pineapple

1/4 cup poppy seeds

1 cup milk

1/2 cup shortening

2/3 cup sugar

1/2 teaspoon vanilla

2 cups flour

2 teaspoons baking powder

1/4 teaspoon salt

2 eggs, beaten

TOPPING:

1/4 cup butter or margarine

1 cup packed brown sugar

1 tablespoon flour

1/2 cup water

1 teaspoon powdered dried orange peel

1 egg, beaten

1/2 pint whipping cream

1 tablespoon sugar

1/2 teaspoon vanilla

Pulverized dried pineapple

Soak powdered dried pineapple and poppy seeds in milk for 15 minutes. Cream together shortening, sugar, and vanilla. In a separate bowl mix flour, baking powder, and salt. Combine half the dry ingredients with the creamed mixture. Add rehydrated pineapple and poppy seeds and the remaining dry ingredients. Mix well. Blend in beaten eggs. Pour into a greased and floured 9-by-13-inch pan. Bake in a 350° F. oven for 35 minutes or until done. Cool cake. To prepare the caramel topping, combine butter or margarine, brown sugar, flour, and water in a saucepan. Add dried orange peel and beaten egg. Mix thoroughly. Cook over medium heat, stirring constantly, until mixture begins to thicken. Remove from heat and cool. Caramel will continue to thicken as it cools. Meanwhile, whip cream. Add sugar and vanilla. Spread cooled caramel on cake, followed by whipped cream. Top with pulverized dried pineapple. Keep refrigerated.

Pineapple-Coconut Cookies

1 cup coarsely chopped dried pineapple
2 tablespoons hot water
3/4 cup butter or margarine
1 cup firmly packed brown sugar
1 egg
2 tablespoons water
1 teaspoon vanilla
1 cup flour
1 teaspoon salt
1/2 teaspoon baking soda
2 cups granola
1 cup flaked dried coconut

Combine pineapple and 2 tablespoons hot water. Set aside. In a large bowl beat together until creamy the butter or margarine, brown sugar, egg, 2 tablespoons water, and vanilla. Stir together flour, salt, and baking soda. Add to creamed mixture. Blend well. Stir in undrained pineapple, granola, and coconut. Drop by teaspoonfuls onto lightly greased baking sheets. Bake in a 350° F. oven for 15 to 18 minutes or until lightly browned.

Easy Pineapple Spice Cake

2/3 cup powdered dried pineapple
2/3 cup apple cider
1/3 cup raisins
1 packaged spice cake mix
Apple-Orange Frosting (page 73)

Soak powdered pineapple in apple cider for 15 minutes. Add raisins. Mix the packaged spice cake according to directions on box. Add rehydrated pineapple and raisins during the last mixing. Let batter sit for 15 minutes. Pour into a greased and floured 9-by-13-inch pan or two 9-inch round cake pans. Bake according to package directions. Cool and frost with Apple-Orange Frosting.

SUBSTITUTIONS
Any flavor cake mix and any dried fruit may be used in place of the spice cake and dried pineapple.

PLUMS/PRUNES

GENERAL INFORMATION

Water content of fresh food:
Damson, 81%; prune plums, 78%; Japanese and hybrid, 87%.

Selection of fresh food for drying:
Over 150 varieties of plums are available, ranging in size from as small as a cherry to as large as a peach. All dry successfully. Select soft and ripe, but not overripe, fruit. Tree-ripened, firm fruit is best. All dried prunes were originally plums, but not all plums dry to become prunes. Prune plums are a special variety which, when dried, are known as prunes. Most other plums, however, are designated as dried plums when dehydrated.

Preparation for drying:
Wash. Do not peel. Cut in half and remove pits. Depending on size, dry cut-side up or cut into ¼- to ½-inch pieces.

Characteristics of dried product:
Pliable for short-term storage, hard yet leathery for long-term storage.

Ways to use:
Use to make preserves and jellies.

Add to desserts, breakfast foods, fruit soups, puddings, cobblers, compotes, and sauces.

Add small pieces to cream cheese or yogurt.

Eat dried as a fast-food snack.

Pulverize and use to sweeten baby food.

Pulverize hard pieces and use the fruit flakes as a flavoring.

RECIPE SUGGESTIONS

Plum/Prune Coffee Cake

1½ cups flour
3 teaspoons baking powder
1 teaspoon salt
1 egg
1/4 cup honey (optional)
1/3 cup oil or melted butter
1 cup milk
1 cup small dried plum or prune pieces
1/4 cup firmly packed brown sugar
2 tablespoons coconut
1 teaspoon cinnamon

Combine flour, baking powder, and salt in a large bowl. In a small bowl lightly beat the egg and add honey, oil or melted butter, and milk. Stir. Add dried plums or prunes. Mix. Combine prune mixture and flour mixture, stirring only enough to moisten the flour. Pour into a lightly greased 9-inch square pan. Combine the brown sugar, coconut, and cinnamon. Sprinkle over batter in pan. Bake in a 375° F. oven for 25 minutes or until done.

SUBSTITUTIONS

Dried apples or combinations such as apple-pear or pear-apricot may be substituted for the plums or prunes.

Apple and Plum Oatmeal Cookies

    1/2 cup very small dried apple pieces
    1/2 cup very small dried plum pieces
    1/2 cup water or fruit juice
    1/2 teaspoon fresh or dried ginger
    1 cup melted butter or margarine
    3/4 cup firmly packed brown sugar
    3/4 cup white sugar
    2 eggs, well beaten
    1 teaspoon vanilla
    1¼ cups white flour
    3/4 cup whole wheat flour
    3 tablespoons bran
    1 teaspoon baking soda
    1 teaspoon salt
    1 teaspoon cinnamon
    1/2 cup oatmeal

Combine dried apples, plums, and water in a small bowl. Add fresh or dried ginger, and let soak 30 minutes. In a large bowl mix melted butter or margarine, brown sugar, and white sugar. Blend. Add well-beaten eggs and vanilla. Stir. Add white flour, whole wheat flour, bran, baking soda, salt, and cinnamon. Mix well. Add oatmeal, rehydrated fruit, plus any remaining liquid. Stir. Let batter rest for 10 minutes. Drop by teaspoonfuls onto a slightly greased cookie sheet. Bake 12 to 15 minutes in a 375° F. oven. Makes 60 cookies.

GENERAL INFORMATION

Water content of fresh food:
81%.

Selection of fresh food for drying:
Both black and red varieties can be dried. Select ripe but not mushy fruit.

Preparation for drying:
Remove any debris. Wash if desired. Place whole berries on trays. (Raspberry leaves may also be dried.)

Characteristics of dried food:
Hard.

Ways to use:
Eat as a snack.

Pulverize and add to gelatins.

Add to breakfast cereals, pancakes, and desserts.

Use to make preserves.

Make raspberry vinegar (see Blueberries, Ways to Use).

Raspberry leaves make excellent tea.

Add leaves to sachets and potpourris.

RECIPE SUGGESTION

Raspberry Pie

    1½ cups dried raspberries
    2 cups water or fruit juice
    1/4 cup honey or maple syrup
    1/2 teaspoon powdered dried orange or lemon peel
    2 tablespoons cornstarch
    1 9-inch double-crust pie pastry (page 27)
    Flour

Soak dried raspberries in water or fruit juice in a saucepan for 15 minutes. Add honey or maple syrup and powdered dried orange or lemon peel. Blend in cornstarch. Mix well. Lightly dust unbaked pie pastry with flour. Pour in raspberry mixture. Place the top pie crust over filling, seal edges, and cut slits to allow steam to escape. Bake 10 minutes in a 425° F. oven. Reduce heat to 325° and bake an additional 20 to 30 minutes or until crust is brown and filling is bubbly.

RHUBARB

GENERAL INFORMATION

Water content of fresh food:
95%.

Selection of fresh food for drying:
Rhubarb is actually a vegetable, but it is used as a fruit. Select fresh, tender stalks that are firm and crisp. Pull up stalks near the base, breaking as close to the base as possible.

Preparation for drying:
Wash and remove any blemished areas. Cut off the pulpy ends. Cut into ½-inch strips or ½-inch cubes. To decrease some of the acidity in the rhubarb and thus reduce the amount of sugar needed to sweeten, pour boiling water over the pieces and let sit for 3 to 5 minutes. Drain.

Characteristics of the dried product:
Brittle.

Ways to use:
Rehydrate and use in pies, cobblers, or preserves.

Rehydrate and serve as a breakfast or dessert fruit.

Add to stewed fruit.

RECIPE SUGGESTIONS

Cherry-Rhubarb Leather
An alternative drying procedure.

1 21-ounce can cherry pie filling

1 cup diced fresh rhubarb

In a small sauce pan cook cherry pie filling and rhubarb until rhubarb is tender, about 10 minutes. Puree in blender. Pour onto two leather sheets.

Rhubarb Sauce

1/2 cup dried rhubarb pieces

2½ cups water

1/4 cup honey

1/2 teaspoon cinnamon

Place rhubarb and 1½ cups water in a 2 quart pan. Let soak 30 minutes. Bring to a boil and cook until rhubarb softens. Stir often. Pour into a blender and puree. Return rhubarb to pan and place remaining 1 cup water in blender. Operate the blender until remaining rhubarb is freed from the blades. Add to rhubarb puree. Add honey and cinnamon. Cook over medium heat until desired thickness. Serve warm or cold. Makes about 2½ cups.

VARIATION
Strawberry-Rhubarb Sauce: Use 1/4 cup dried strawberry pieces and 1/4 cup dried rhubarb pieces. Follow directions for Rhubarb Sauce.

STRAWBERRIES

GENERAL INFORMATION

Water content of fresh food:
90%.

Selection of fresh food for drying:
Choose ripe but firm strawberries that are free of blemishes. Avoid woody and soft strawberries.

Preparation for drying:
Remove any stem or leafy parts. (Strawberry leaves can also be dried.) Remove caps. Wash if necessary. Strawberries can be dried whole if small, cut in half, or into ½-inch pieces.

Characteristics of dried product:
Firm for short-term storage, hard for long-term storage.

Ways to use:
Pulverize and sprinkle on fruit salads, and yogurt.

Add to dry or cooked breakfast cereals.

Enjoy dried strawberries as a snack.

Rehydrate and use in jello, sauces, desserts, pies, cobblers, and pancakes.

RECIPE SUGGESTIONS

Strawberry Meringue Cookies

4 egg whites

1/4 teaspoon salt

1 teaspoon cream of tartar

1 cup sugar

1/2 teaspoon vanilla

1/4 cup pulverized dried strawberries

Beat egg whites until frothy. Sprinkle salt and cream of tartar over egg whites and continue beating. When egg whites are almost stiff, gradually add the sugar, approximately 2 tablespoons at a time, beating constantly. Add the vanilla and pulverized dried strawberries. Egg whites should be very stiff. Drop by heaping tablespoonfuls onto a heavily greased cookie sheet. Bake in a 250° to 275° F. oven for 45 to 60 minutes or until lightly browned and very dry. Yields about 8 dozen.

SUBSTITUTIONS
Other berries or pulverized dried fruits can be used in place of the strawberries.

Flaky Strawberry Phyllo Pastries (page 88)

Strawberry Ice Cream

2 cups dried strawberry pieces
1½ cups lukewarm water
3/4 cup sugar
1/3 cup water
1 tablespoon light corn syrup
2 egg whites
1/2 cup whipping cream
2-3 drops red food coloring (optional)

Combine strawberries and 1½ cups water. Let stand 1 hour, stirring occasionally. Pour into blender and puree until smooth. Set aside. Combine sugar, 1/3 cup water, and corn syrup in a small saucepan. Cook over medium heat, stirring constantly, until sugar is dissolved, then bring to a boil without stirring. Boil until mixture reaches soft-ball stage— 234° to 240° on a candy thermometer or until a small amount spooned into ice water can be molded into a soft ball. Meanwhile, beat egg whites until stiff but not dry. In a separate bowl beat cream until soft peaks form. When sugar mixture reaches soft-ball stage, remove from heat immediately. Slowly pour into egg whites, beating constantly on high speed of electric mixer. Continue beating until mixture is thick and shiny. Fold strawberry puree into whipped cream. Gradually pour strawberry mixture into egg whites, beating slowly to blend. Add food coloring, if desired. Pour into loaf pan or 1½-quart container. Cover with plastic wrap and freeze. Ice cream may also be frozen in a churn-type freezer. Makes 1¼ quarts.

VARIATION

Quick Strawberry Ice Cream: Combine 1/2 cup dried strawberries and 1/2 cup lukewarm water. Let stand 1 hour. Puree in blender. Add 1/4 pint softened vanilla ice cream. Blend well. Add remaining 3/4 pint vanilla ice cream. Blend just enough to mix. Freeze. Makes 1 pint.

Strawberry Phyllo Pastries (Pictured on page 87)

2 cups apple cider or orange juice
2 heaping tablespoons cornstarch
1 cup dried strawberries
1 cup butter or margarine
1 cup honey
1 teaspoon cinnamon (optional)
1 teaspoon dried orange peel (optional)
1 1-pound package phyllo

Mix apple cider or orange juice and cornstarch in a small saucepan. Stir until no lumps remain. Add dried strawberries and let sit 1 hour. Simmer over medium heat until mixture thickens. In another small saucepan, heat butter or margarine and honey. Add cinnamon and dried orange peel, if desired. Unfold the phyllo pastry and cut the entire stack into fourths. Dough should be rectangular in shape. Spread about 1 teaspoon of the honey-butter mixture on top of two sheets phyllo dough. Place two more sheets on top and spread with an additional teaspoon honey-butter. Repeat once more. Dough should be six layers thick. Place 2 tablespoons of the cooked strawberries in the center of the phyllo squares. Fold into triangles, tucking ends so that filling does not leak out. Place on a cookie sheet, brush tops with honey-butter mixture, and bake in 375° to 400° F. oven for 20 minutes or until golden brown. Makes 10 to 12 pastries.

SUBSTITUTIONS

Raspberries, bananas, peaches, grapes, papayas, blueberries, or any combination of dried fruits may be substituted for the strawberries.

MEATS

Meats, poultry, and fish dry beautifully in the Magic Aire II. The resulting products are lightweight and high in protein, making them an ideal food for outdoor enthusiasts. The dehydrator turns thin slices of beef, poultry, fish, or game meats into hearty midafternoon snacks or food to use much like salami on pizza or hash for main dishes. By taking advantage of fresh meat specials, these dried products can be obtained for a fraction of the cost of commercially prepared dried meats.

There are many different types of dried meat and fish. Smoking and curing are ancient yet commonly practiced commercial methods of retarding bacterial growth. Home smoking and curing, however, require special techniques and equipment. The Magic Aire II can be used to make jerky and dried meat. Jerky is raw meat or fish which has been seasoned and dried. Dried meat refers to meat, poultry, or fish which has been cooked then dried. All jerky is dried meat, but not all dried meat is jerky.

Practically any meat can be dried, but fatty meats are not recommended. It is also not advised to dry fresh pork for jerky as the drying temperature is not high enough to kill the harmful bacteria. Choose lean cuts of meat. Beef flank, round, or rump cuts are better than rib or chuck. Chicken breasts are more lean than dark meat. Some fish have a higher fat content than others; sole and flounder are good choices. It is important to use lean meats, poultry, and fish as fat turns rancid during storage.

Preparation
Cut meats across the grain into thin strips about 1-inch wide and ¼-inch thick. Trim off all fat and connective tissues. For easier cutting, partially freeze by placing meats on the bottom of the freezer for about 30 minutes. Turn and freeze 15 minutes longer. To prepare fish, filet, then cut into 1-inch strips. See cutting instructions under Fish (page 94).

JERKY
To prepare beef, venison, or fish jerky, begin with a clean cutting surface. Cleanliness is most essential when working with raw meats.

After meat or fish is trimmed, it may be seasoned or marinated. Any one or more of the following seasonings may be used: garlic powder, onion powder, salt or soy sauce, Worcestershire sauce, Tabasco sauce or pepper, paprika, ginger, oregano, basil, marjoram, rosemary, thyme, or curry powder. Seasonings can be sprinkled on or pounded into meat with a hammer or a mallet. Because flavors intensify with dehydration, use salt sparingly. However, season meat for jerky a little heavier than for regular cooking.

Meats and fish can also be marinated in liquids from ½ hour to overnight in the refrigerator. A simple salt solution marinade improves flavor while it reduces the potential of spoilage. Most barbecue marinades may be used, as long as they contain no oil. A soy or teriyaki marinade makes for a particularly delicious jerky. For stronger flavors, add additional seasonings and increase marinating time. Adding lemon juice to a meat marinade will help preserve redness. When marinating poultry, use lemon or orange juice to add flavor. Vinegar added to a marinate will soften the wild taste of game meats. Before placing meats and fish on drying trays, drain off any excess marinade and blot dry with paper toweling.

DRIED MEATS
Poultry is generally cooked before drying as the flavor and texture are much improved by cooking. Meats and fish may also be cooked, then dried. Braising, pot roasting, or steaming are the best methods of cooking because there is no need to add fat. Meats may be seasoned or marinated before cooking, or seasoned after cooking and before drying. Detailed instructions are given on the pages which follow.

Teriyaki Marinade (Pictured on page 92)
   1/3 cup Kikkoman Teriyaki Barbecue Marinade and Sauce
   2 bay leaves
   12 peppercorns
   1/4 teaspoon Tabasco sauce
   1/2 teaspoon garlic powder
   2 teaspoons Worcestershire sauce

Combine all ingredients. (Use to marinate fresh or cooked meat, poultry, or fish.)

Soy Marinade
   1/4 cup soy sauce
   2 tablespoons honey
   1/2 teaspoon dry mustard
   1/4 teaspoon garlic powder

Combine all ingredients. (Use to marinate fresh or cooked meat, poultry, or fish.)

Drying Time
Meats, poultry, and fish generally take 6 to 12 hours to dry. Dehydrate until pieces are dry but will bend without breaking. Jerky should be slightly chewy, not brittle, with no evidence of moisture. Dehydrated meats, poultry, and fish darken in color when dried.

Storing

Dried meats, poultry, and fish deteriorate quickly in flavor, so do not dry them for long-term storage, but they can be most satisfactorily dried for upcoming camping and backpacking trips. Storage of longer than 2 months is not suggested. Keep dried products in an airtight container, a sealed plastic bag, or a jar with an airtight lid. For insured safety, keep in the refrigerator or freezer.

Rehydration

Rehydration is usually completed in 1 to 4 hours by soaking in an equal amount of water or by gently simmering in water. Use only enough water to cover the product. Reconstitution yields a tasty product, not unlike the fresh which has been cooked.

BEEF

GENERAL INFORMATION

Water content of fresh food:
69%.

Selection of fresh food for drying:
Choose a flank, rump, brisket, or round cut. The leaner the meat, the better the quality of the dried product.

Preparation for drying:
Method 1: Cook as for pot roast. Remove all fat. Chill. Cut into ½-inch cubes or strips. Sprinkle with desired seasonings, place on dehydrator trays, and dry.

Method 2: Slice meat into 2- to 3-inch strips about ½-inch thick, cutting across the grain. Trim off fat. Marinate, or season with salt, pepper, and herbs. Place on drying trays. Turn meat at least once while drying.

Method 3: Slice meat into 2- to 3-inch strips about ½-inch thick, cutting across the grain. Trim off fat. Soak strips in a solution of 2 quarts water and ½ cup salt for a minimum of 2 hours. Keep refrigerated. (Soaking reduces the potential of spoilage.) Remove from brine and drain. Place strips on tray, and turn periodically during drying.

Method 4: Chill meat in the freezer for about 1 hour before cutting. Slice and proceed as in Methods 2 or 3.

Characteristics of dried product:
Leathery to brittle.

Ways to use:
Enjoy as a high-protein snack.

Add to soups or stews.

Slice and add to pizza.

Use creamed in cooking.

Serve with cheese and crackers.

Add to casseroles and gravies.

Teriyaki Jerky
An alternative drying procedure.

    1 large bay leaf
    1 pound raw lean beef strips
    1/2 cup Kikkoman Teriyaki Barbecue Marinade and
        Sauce

Place bay leaf in the bottom of a flat dish or bowl. Add meat and Teriyaki Barbecue Marinade. Cover and refrigerate 12 hours, turning meat often. Drain and place strips on dehydrator trays. Dry until hard.

Creamed Beef and Cheese

    3/4 cup very small dried beef pieces
    1 cup water
    1/4 cup butter or margarine
    1/4 cup flour
    2 cups milk
    1 cup grated cheese
    Boiled potatoes, cooked noodles, or English muffins

Soak dried beef pieces in water for 1 hour. Drain. Melt butter or margarine in a small saucepan. Add drained beef, and saute. Stir in flour. Cook and stir over medium heat for 2 to 3 minutes. Add milk and cook until thickened. Remove from heat. Blend in grated cheese and serve over boiled potatoes, cooked noodles, or English muffins. Serves 4 to 6.

FISH

GENERAL INFORMATION

Water content of fresh food:
65% (approximate).

Selection of fresh food for drying:
Cod, flounder, halibut, and sole are the most commonly used fish for dehydration, but any kind can be dried. Select lean fish that are easily boned. Other varieties to dry include bass, catfish, haddock, perch, pike, salmon, snapper, trout, walleye pike, whitefish, and whiting.

Preparation for drying:
To minimize the chance of spoilage, clean the fish, wash with fresh water, and put on ice or in the refrigerator as soon as possible after catching. To prepare for drying, scale if necessary. Remove skin and head, but leave the collarbone. Split the fish along the backbone and remove backbone. Cut the sides into long, 1-inch strips. Remove the collarbone, and wash strips thoroughly.

Method 1: Soak strips in a solution of 2 quarts water and 1 cup salt for a minimum of 8 hours.

Seasonings, such as peppercorns, lemon juice, or dill, can be added to the salt brine. Keep refrigerated. Remove from brine and drain. Sprinkle with 1 to 2 teaspoons of seasonings, such as lemon juice, soy sauce, Tabasco sauce, paprika, salt, pepper, powdered garlic, powdered onion, sugar, or dill. Place on dehydrator trays and dry.

Method 2: Place fish strips in a steamer and steam over boiling water until tender. Sprinkle with seasonings as described in Method 1. Place on dehydrator trays and dry.

Characteristics of dried product:
Dry and tough.

Ways to use:
Eat as a snack.

Add to dried camper stews.

Rehydrate and use in chowders and soups.

Add dried to canapes and serve with crackers.

RECIPE SUGGESTIONS

Fish Chowder

    3/4 cup very small dried fish pieces
    1½ cups water
    1 teaspoon dried dill weed
    1/4 cup diced fresh green bell pepper
    1/4 cup diced fresh onion
    3 cups cubed fresh potatoes
    1/2 cup sliced fresh celery
    1 cup sliced fresh carrots
    3 cups water
    3 tablespoons butter
    3 tablespoons flour
    1½ cups milk
    1 teaspoon dried rosemary
    1/4 cup cooking sherry or 1 lemon, juiced
    Hard boiled egg slices
    Paprika or dried parsley

Soak dried fish pieces in 1½ cups water in a large pot for 30 minutes. Add dried dill weed, green bell pepper, and onion. Cook until fish is soft. In another pan cook potatoes, celery, and carrots in 3 cups water until tender. In a third pan melt butter, add flour, and cook 2 to 3 minutes. Add milk and rosemary. Cook until thickened. Mix the cooked vegetables and water with the fish. Add creamed sauce. Heat through. Add cooking sherry or lemon juice 2 minutes before removing from heat. Garnish with hard boiled egg slices and paprika or dried parsley. Serves 8.

SUBSTITUTIONS
Dried vegetables may be substituted for the fresh. Soak with fish to reconstitute, adding additional water.

Fish Casserole

1/2 cup very small dried fish pieces
1 cup water
1 10¾-ounce can cream of mushroom soup
2 cups cooked noodles
1 17-ounce can peas, drained
Pepper
1/2 cup grated cheese

In a casserole dish soak dried fish pieces in water for 1 hour. Drain. Add cream of mushroom soup, cooked noodles, and peas. Stir. Pepper to taste. Top with grated cheese. Cover and bake in a 350° F. oven for 45 minutes. Uncover and bake an additional 10 minutes. Serves 4.

POULTRY

GENERAL INFORMATION

Water content of fresh food:
Chicken (without skin), 64%; turkey (fresh), 61%.

Selection of fresh food for drying:
Fresh or frozen poultry may be used. Chicken and turkey are best as they contain less fat than other birds.

Preparation for drying:
Cook by steaming or roasting. Remove all fat and skin. Cool. Separate meat from bones. Cut or break into ½- to 2-inch pieces or cubes. If desired, sprinkle with seasonings.

Characteristics of dried product:
Hard.

Ways to use:
Add to stews, casseroles, and soups.

Add to dried soups and stews for backpacking and camping.

Enjoy as a high-protein snack.

Marinated Chicken
An alternative drying procedure.

1 3-4 pound cut-up chicken
1/2 cup soy sauce
1/2 cup vinegar
1 cup water
1 lemon, juiced
1 bay leaf
6 peppercorns
2 tablespoons chopped onion
1 teaspoon dried basil or oregano
Salt and pepper

Remove skin and fat from chicken pieces. Combine remaining ingredients in a small saucepan and simmer over low heat 2 to 3 minutes or until flavors blend. Pour over chicken pieces and let sit in refrigerator 8 hours, turning often. Bake chicken in marinade in a 350° F. oven for 40 to 45 minutes or until tender. Remove meat from bones. Cut into desired size, place on dehydrator trays, and dry.

Chicken/Turkey Fried Rice

1/2 cup very small dried chicken or turkey pieces
2 tablespoons dried onion
3/4 cup water
2 cups uncooked rice
4 cups water
2-4 tablespoons butter or margarine
Salt and pepper

In a small saucepan soak dried chicken or turkey pieces and dried onion in ¾ cup water for 1 hour. Cook until soft, adding more liquid during cooking if necessary. Drain. In a separate pan, cook rice in 4 cups water until tender and water is absorbed. Melt butter or margarine in a large skillet. Saute rehydrated poultry and onions. Add rice and cook until golden brown. Season to taste with salt and pepper. Serves 6 to 8.

VARIATIONS
Curry powder may be added for additional flavor. The recipe may be prepared by combining all ingredients in a slow cooker and cooking on low for 4 hours.

SHRIMP

GENERAL INFORMATION

Water content of fresh food:
70%.

Selection of fresh food for drying:
Fresh or frozen shrimp can be dehydrated. Dehydrating shrimp is commonly practiced in the southern Gulf states and throughout the Orient.

Preparation for drying:
Thaw frozen shrimp. Place shrimp in a rapidly boiling salt solution of 2 quarts water and ½ cup salt. After the water returns to a boil, cook shrimp 1 to 3 minutes, depending on size. Shrimp will turn pink. Remove, drain, and shell. Shrimp may be cut into smaller pieces before placing on drying trays.

Characteristics of dried product:
Hard.

Ways to use:
Add to soups or chowders.

Add to casserole and creoles.

Rehydrate small pieces, mix with creamed cheese and seasonings, and spread on crackers.

Rehydrate and add to salads.

RECIPE SUGGESTIONS

Shrimp and Noodles

1/4 cup boiling water
20 dried shrimp
1 1½-inch piece fresh ginger root
1/8 teaspoon pepper
2 cucumbers
3 tablespoons oil
1½ teaspoons salt
1 cup chicken broth
2 ounces Chinese egg noodles

Pour boiling water over dried shrimp. Using a garlic press, squeeze the ginger root into the rehydrating shrimp. Add pepper. Let sit 1 hour. Peel the cucumbers. Cut diagonally into ¼-inch slices, then into ¼-inch strips. Measure 3 cups. Set aside. Drain shrimp, reserving any remaining liquid. Heat oil in a skillet. When hot, fry rehydrated shrimp for 2 minutes. Add cucumber strips and stir fry 1 minute. Add the shrimp water, salt, and chicken broth. Break noodles into 4-inch pieces and add. Cook over low heat until noodles are soft, approximately 10 minutes. Serves 2.

Shrimp Egg Rolls

1/2 cup small dried shrimp pieces
1/4 cup water
1 small head cabbage
Cooking oil
1 pound fresh bean sprouts
1 cup chopped fresh celery
1 tablespoon sugar
1 teaspoon salt
1/4 teaspoon pepper
1 8-ounce can bamboo shoots, drained and diced
1 8-ounce can water chestnuts, drained and diced
1 2-ounce jar pimento
20 egg roll skins, thawed
Deep-fat cooking oil
Sweet and Sour Sauce (recipe below) or Hot Pepper Jelly (page 43)

Soak dried shrimp in water for 1 hour. Dice cabbage. Cover the bottom of a large frying pan or wok with ¼ inch of cooking oil. Stir in cabbage, bean sprouts, and celery, coating evenly with oil. Add sugar, salt, and pepper. Drain shrimp and add. Cover and steam 2 to 3 minutes. Cool. Add drained and diced bamboo shoots, water chestnuts, and pimento. Pour mixture into a strainer or colander, and press to extract liquid. Place 2½ to 3 tablespoons filling in the center of each egg roll skin. Roll and seal. Deep-fat fry until brown. Serve with Sweet and Sour Sauce or Hot Pepper Jelly. Makes 20 egg rolls.

VARIATION
Other dried vegetables, such as mushrooms, green pepper, or onion, may be added during steaming.

Sweet and Sour Sauce

1/4 cup dried pineapple pieces
3/4 cup water
3 tablespoons cooking oil
1 tablespoon soy sauce
1/4 cup vinegar
1/4 teaspoon dried ginger
2 tablespoons sugar
1 teaspoon cornstarch

Combine the first seven ingredients in a small saucepan. Cook until pineapple softens. Place in blender and puree. Add cornstarch, and blend again. Return to pan and cook over medium heat until mixture thickens.

VENISON

GENERAL INFORMATION

Water content of fresh food:
74%.

Selection of fresh food for drying:
The loin, round, tenderloin, and flank are best, but any cut can be used. Use lean pieces and remove all fat or connecting tissue which may turn rancid after drying.

Preparation for drying:
Method 1: Use the lean pieces and trim all excess fat. Cut into 1- to 2-inch strips about ½-inch thick. Soak the strips in a solution of 1 quart water and ½ cup salt for a minimum of 8 hours. Keep refrigerated. Remove and drain. Place on trays. Turn strips periodically during drying.

Method 2: Prepare as in Method 1. After removing from salt solution, marinate with Teriyaki Marinade or Soy Marinade (page 91) for several hours. Juniper berries, peppercorns, basil, or vinegar may be added to the marinade. (Vinegar helps diminish the wild taste.) Place on trays and dry.

Method 3: Use lean pieces and trim all fat. Cut into 1- to 2-inch strips about ½-inch thick. Place in a steamer and steam over boiling water until all redness disappears. (This procedure is recommended by some drying authorities as a precaution against trichinosis.) Season to taste with salt, pepper, and spices. Place on trays and dry.

Characteristics of dried product:
Brittle and tough.

Ways to use:
Eat as a snack and protein treat.

Add to soups, stews, and casseroles.

Combine with eggs.

RECIPE SUGGESTIONS

Venison Jerky
An alternative drying procedure.

    1/4 cup cider vinegar
    4 tablespoons Worcestershire sauce
    2 tablespoons brown sugar
    1 teaspoon salt
    1 teaspoon dried garlic powder
    1/2 teaspoon pepper
    1-2 pounds raw lean venison strips

Place all ingredients in a flat dish or bowl. Cover and refrigerate 8 hours or overnight, turning often. Drain and place strips on dehydrator trays. Dry until hard.

Pemmican

    1½ cups diced dried venison
    1 cup peanut butter
    1/2 cup dried blueberries
    1/2 cup raisins
    1/2 cup small dried apple pieces

Combine all ingredients and shape into 1-inch balls. (Serve as a snack or pack for outdoor outings. Four balls and a handful of rose hips provide sustenance for a day.) Makes 18 balls.

HERBS

Drying your own herbs can be one of the most rewarding, creative, and economical aspects of owning a Magic Aire II Food Dehydrator. Plus growing, harvesting, drying, and using herbs is far easier than most people believe.

If dried quickly and stored properly, dried herbs are two to three times more flavorful than fresh herbs. Quick-drying is desirable because it captures the full food value, preserves the oils, and maintains good color, whereas valuable nutrients and flavor are lost if a slow-drying process is used. There should be no taste difference between fresh and dried herbs.

Herbs are best harvested on a sunny morning after the dew has evaporated. Gather herbs just before the plant blooms—the time when plants are richest in the oils that give herbs their special flavor and aroma. Many herbs can be harvested throughout the entire growing season. You may cut up to two-thirds of the plant, leaving the rest to grow. Once plants are cut, regular cuttings will prevent them from flowering.

Dried herbs have an excellent shelf life. According to *Naturalife News*, published by Naturalife International, Inc., Orem, Utah: "The stability of dried herbs has been proven through history and through modern scientific testings. Dried herbs, if stored under normal storage conditions, i.e., at 75-80 degrees F. in a dark and dry place and in an airtight container, will keep their freshness and potency for four years or more (some up to six to eight years), conservatively speaking." It is best to store herbs in a dark glass jar, away from the light, as light will cause the color to fade. Remember to label the jars—dried herbs can be difficult to distinguish from one another.

Dried herbs can be used in a wide variety of ways. Flavoring foods—soups, sauces, meats, desserts, and salads—is the most popular. Dried herbs are excellent in drinks, butters, vinegars, mustards, jams, jellies, preserves, dressings, baths, potpourris, and sachets. They can also be added to floral arrangements. Herbs do not need to be rehydrated before using, but soaking in a small amount of oil, liqueur, or water will intensify the flavor of some herbs.

Preparation
Select herbs in prime condition (before they turn brown, old, or woody). The leaves should be fully developed, yet tender. Herbs do not require any pretreatment, but be sure to remove any brown spots and insect debris from the leaves, and to strip off the leaves from the larger stems. If the leaves are dirty, wash in cold water and spread on absorbent toweling to dry, dust with a clean, damp cloth, or shake the plants. If using wild herbs, make sure the plant has not been sprayed with chemicals.

Most herbs can be placed on the drying trays within minutes of picking and cleaning, and they will dry in approximately 2 hours. When drying small pieces of food that may fall through the trays, use the sprouting tray inserts or leather sheets, or collect the pieces from the base unit. Herbs are brittle when dry. Some leaves will darken in color, but darkening does not affect flavor. After drying, leaves can be left whole, stripped from the stem, or crushed. To prepare for storage and kitchen use, dried herbs can be pressed through a fine screen, powdered with a mortar and pestle, or rubbed between your fingers.

Herb Drinks
Hot teas or cold beverages can be made from a single herb or from a combination of several herbs and spices. Herbal teas do not contain tannin or caffeine which are found in other teas and coffee.

For hot teas, pour approximately 1 cup of boiling water over 1 teaspoon of dried herbs to make 1 cup of tea. Hot water releases the fragrance and flavor of dried herbs. When making a pot of tea, use 1 teaspoon of herbs for each cup of water, plus an extra teaspoon of herbs. In the winter, warm the teacups and the teapot before pouring in the hot water. A tea cozy also works well when brewing herbal teas. Allow the brew to steep for 3 to 8 minutes. Stronger teas need to steep longer. If the water is not hot enough, the leaves will float instead of sinking to the bottom. Taste the tea to see if it is strong enough. Sweeten with honey, maple syrup, or sugar.

To use herbs for iced teas, pour 1 cup hot water over 1½ teaspoons dried herbs to make 1 cup of tea. Herb iced tea should be made stronger than hot tea because the flavor of the tea will be diluted by the melting ice. Place the tea in a clear jar and allow it to steep in a warm, not hot, place. To make sun tea, put tea in hot water and place in the sun. After several hours (this time varies according to the flavor of the tea), strain the tea to remove the herbs. Place ice cubes in the tea and chill until serving time. Sweeten with honey, maple syrup, or sugar.

Experiment with different herbs and different combinations of herbs. Several different herbs, such as mint and camomile or raspberry and dandelion flowers, can be used together. Pieces of dried fruit, such as dried lemon or orange peel, can be added to the steeping tea. Add other flavorings, including cinnamon, anise seeds, or whole cloves, to make new and interesting beverages.

Herb teas can be made into ice cubes and floated in punches, iced teas, or added to fruit drinks.

Herb Butters

Herb butters are butters or margarines that are flavored with herbs. These butters are used to enhance many different foods. Single herbs or herb combinations, such as chives, parsley, oregano, basil, thyme, and rosemary, can be used. Dried lemon peel, garlic powder, or onion powder can also be added to flavor herb butters.

To make herb butters, heat 1/4 pound of butter or margarine and add 1½ teaspoons dried herbs. The flavor of herb butters varies according to the amount of herbs added; add a little at a time, tasting often, until you obtain the flavor you like. Refrigerate herb butters 1 to 2 hours to allow flavors to mellow before serving. Herb butters can be frozen and used as needed.

Spread herb butters on breads, glaze cooked vegetables, or dot on meat. You can also use herb butters to fry foods, especially eggs, and to flavor sauces and cream soups.

Basic Herb Butter

Used by permission of *Herb Forum*.

> 1/2 cup butter or margarine, softened
>
> 1 tablespoon lemon juice
>
> 1 tablespoon crushed dried herbs*
>
> Salt and pepper

*Suggested herbs include marjoram, dill, oregano and basil, and tarragon.

In a small bowl cream butter or margarine. Slowly add lemon juice. Add herbs, and salt and pepper to taste. Cover and refrigerate.

Herb Vinegars

Herb vinegars are made by adding dried herbs to vinegar. Herbs soften the sharp flavor of vinegar. Try basil, mint, or garlic, or use a combination of your favorite herbs. Basil vinegar gives a nice accent to salad dressings, and mint vinegar enhances the flavor of fruit salads. Use herb vinegars to flavor meat marinades, soups, stews, sauces, deviled eggs, and gravies. Wine vinegar is generally preferred as a base, but any good white or red vinegar will do. Malt vinegar and cider vinegar can be used to make herb vinegars; however, cider vinegar has a strong flavor which may mask the subtle flavor of some delicate herbs. Garlic, chives, basil, mint, and tarragon are strong herbs which are suitable for use with cider vinegar. Dried lemon or orange peel, flower heads, cloves, dried fruits, dried vegetables, garlic, and spices are also added to season herb vinegars.

To make herb vinegars, place 1/2 cup dried herbs in a clear glass container and pour 2 cups vinegar over the herbs. Some herb users suggest pouring warm vinegar over the herbs because the heat helps to extract the oils and to release the flavor from the dried herbs more quickly than does cool vinegar. Adjust the proportion of herbs to individual taste. The stronger the flavor of the herb, the less you need. If using herb combinations, stronger herbs may overpower the flavor of more delicate herbs, so adjust proportions accordingly.

Allow the herb vinegar to sit in the sun or in another warm place to give the vinegar time to infuse the flavor of the herbs. Occasionally, gently shake the bottle. After 1 or 2 weeks, taste the vinegar. If the flavor is too weak, let the vinegar rest for another week or add more herbs. If the herb vinegar is too strong, just add more vinegar. Herb vinegar can be strained after it reaches the desired flavor. When straining and bottling, always use glass, porcelain, or stainless steel equipment to avoid a chemical reaction from the acid. If you do not strain the vinegar, you may be able to identify the type by viewing the herbs, but it's best to label the bottle and to date it.

Herb Mustards

Dried herbs, such as basil, tarragon, dill, rosemary, or sage, added to prepared mustards create exciting, new mustard flavors. Add 1 tablespoon of the crushed dried herb of your choice to 8 ounces of prepared mustard. Dried herbs can also be added to homemade mustards, such as the one that follows.

Hot Sweet Mustard

> 1/4 cup dry mustard
>
> 2/3 cup water
>
> 1½ tablespoons cornstarch
>
> 1/4 cup sugar
>
> 1/2 teaspoon salt
>
> 1/3 cup vinegar

In a small bowl mix mustard with 1/4 cup of the water. Allow to stand. In a small saucepan mix cornstarch, sugar, and salt with remaining water. Add vinegar. Cook over low heat. With a wire whisk, stir constantly until thickened. Remove from heat. Cool. Stir in mustard mixture. (The amount of mustard used will determine the hotness of the product. For a milder mustard, add less of the mustard mixture.) Yields 1 cup.

Herb Jellies, Jams, and Preserves

Dried herbs and jellies, jams, preserves, marmalades, and conserves make wonderful combinations. Try adding dried mint to pineapple jam, thyme to grapefruit jelly, oregano to orange jelly, thyme to citrus marmalade, and camomile or rose geranium to apple jelly. Since dried herbs are two to three times more potent than fresh herbs, add herbs sparingly. Dry your herbs and fruits during the growing season. Then when the weather is cold, when you want the heat and moisture in your home, and when you have the time and energy, bring out your dried foods and fill your home with the wonderful aroma of homemade jams and jellies.

Singular herb jellied products are made by substituting any dried herb in place of the mint in a mint jelly recipe. A basic herb jelly recipe follows. Herbs may also be added to the clear juice of fruits which is used for making jellies. Strain after the dried herbs have had time to flavor the liquid. The use of commercial pectin or high-pectin fruits is essential to obtain a satisfactory jellied product.

Herb Jelly

2 cups water
1 cup white vinegar
6½ cups sugar
1/2-3/4 cup dried herbs*
Food coloring (optional)
1 6-ounce bottle liquid fruit pectin

Combine water, vinegar, and sugar in a large saucepan. Add dried herbs. Tint with food coloring, if desired. Bring to a boil. Add pectin. Heat to full rolling boil, and boil 1 minute. Remove herbs. Pour liquid into hot, sterilized jars and seal. Makes 7 cups.

*Suggested herbs include mint, basil, lavender, rose geranium, tarragon, rose petals, rose hips, rosemary, sage, thyme, and sweet marjoram.

For jams, add dried herbs to the fruit before bottling, or cook the dried herbs along with the fruit. Place a sprig of herb in preserves, along with the large pieces of fruit. In marmalades, crushed dried herbs can be mixed with the small pieces of fruit. Herbs may be added to the citrus fruits, nuts, and raisins of conserves to enhance their flavor. For easy identification of herb jellies, jams, and preserves, place a dried sprig of the accent herb into the jar before pouring in the product.

Remember, honey can be substituted for sugar when making jellied products. Honey gives the jellied product a stronger flavor and color.

Herb Salts

Herb salts can be made from many dried herbs: basil, garlic, parsley, and oregano, to name a few. Simply add equal parts of crushed dried herbs and salt. Coarse salt, such as kosher salt, adds more texture. Store salts in a jar, label, and use to season foods as desired. Herb salts are one way of cutting down salt intake without sacrificing flavor. Even the simplest dishes—rice, noodles, and potatoes—come alive with the flavor of herb salts.

Culinary Salts
Used by permission of *Herb Forum*.

FOR PORK DISHES:
1 cup kosher salt
8 teaspoons dried sage
8 teaspoons crushed dried marjoram

FOR CHICKEN DISHES:
1 cup kosher salt
8 teaspoons dried rosemary
4 teaspoons crushed dried thyme
4 teaspoons dried lemon balm

Blend ingredients. For a finer salt, whirl in blender. Label and store.

Herb Seasoned Salt

3/4 cup salt
1 teaspoon dried thyme
1 teaspoon dried oregano
1 teaspoon dried garlic powder
2 teaspoons paprika
2 teaspoons dry mustard
1/2 teaspoon curry powder
1 teaspoon powdered dried bell pepper
1 teaspoon powdered dried onion
1/2 teaspoon powdered dried celery

Blend all ingredients. Label and store. (Use as a seasoning in eggs, poultry, pork, gravies, salads, or sauces.) Makes 1¼ cups.

Herb Breads
Sprinkle a handful of dried herbs or seeds into the bread dough while kneading. Bake as usual.

Herb Blends
Bouquet garnis and fines herbes are two of the formal and commonly recognized herb blends, although there are any number of ways to informally blend herbs. When combining herbs, the goal is to create a harmonious blend. A bouquet garnis is a mixture combining at least three dried herbs. Herbs are placed in a muslin or cheesecloth bag, tied closed, and used to flavor stews, soups, broths, seafoods, and sauces. Several different kinds of bouquet garnis can be prepared at one time for easy use and accessibility throughout the year. Remember to label each one.

Most bouquet garnis use a bay leaf as a central ingredient, with parsley, thyme, basil, savory, rosemary, lovage, oregano, sweet marjoram, and chives added to make many exciting combinations. Bouquet garnis often have one ingredient from the parsley, the onion, and the mint families. Dried lemon peel, peppercorns, whole cloves, dried onions, and dried celery leaves can be added to accent the herbal mixture. To a basic, traditional mixture of 1 bay leaf, 1/2 cup dried parsley flakes, and 1/4 cup dried thyme leaves, add other herbs to create different flavors for various dishes.

To prepare a bouquet garni, select the dried herbs you wish to use. Place the dried herbs on a 3- to 4-inch square of muslin or cheesecloth, and gather up the sides of the cloth around the herbs. Tie the cloth closed with string, leaving enough string from the cloth bag to easily raise and lower the bouquet garni from the cooking pot. Bouquet garnis are generally added to foods at the beginning of the cooking process and removed before serving.

Bouquet Garni

    1 dried bay leaf
    1 tablespoon dried parsley
    1 teaspoon dried rosemary
    1 teaspoon dried thyme
    1 teaspoon dried tarragon (optional)
    1 small, leafy celery tip

Combine all ingredients and enclose in a muslin or cheesecloth bag.

A bouquet garni for the bath can be made by enclosing a couple of tablespoons of dried herbs and flowers in a cloth bag. Tie the bouquet garni over the faucet so that bathwater filters through the bag, or soak the herbs in a pitcher of water and pour the water into the tub. Use sage, thyme, rosemary, mint, lavender, basil, or marjoram.

Fines herbes, which mean finely chopped, are made from parsley and chives in combination with two or more dried herbs, such as chervil, basil, thyme, rosemary, sweet marjoram, oregano, sage, and tarragon. Fines herbes are used to flavor white sauces and cream soups; accent vegetables, fish and chicken; enhance egg dishes; enliven sour cream; and add exquisite flavors to dips and cream cheese.

Fines Herbes

    1/4 cup crushed dried parsley
    1/4 cup crushed dried chervil
    1/4 cup crushed dried chives
    1/4 cup crushed dried tarragon

Combine all ingredients and store in an airtight container. Makes 1 cup.

Other dried herb combinations can be made and added to flavor foods. Blend equal parts of two or three herbs, such as basil, rosemary, and oregano to flavor tomato dishes, or blend equal parts of chives and parsley to flavor eggs. For flavoring meats and stews, blend 2 teaspoons dried thyme, 1 teaspoon dried basil, and 1 teaspoon dried parsley. Use 2 teaspoons parsley, 1 teaspoon tarragon, and 1 teaspoon chervil for flavoring sauces.

Flowers

The sweet fragrance of flowers can be captured indefinitely through dehydration with the Magic Aire II Food Dehydrator. The aroma of dehydrating flowers adds a lovely scent to the home. Experiment with drying flowers in your dehydrator and develop specialties that are distinctively your own.

Select fully formed flower blossoms which have not yet reached their peak. Cut flowers in the morning after the dew has evaporated and before the sun is high. Avoid watering flowers before picking, and do not pick them after a rainfall. If possible, collect the flowers the day they open—the time when the blossoms are at their best. Fresh flowers hold their color better and do not fall apart. If flowers have reached the seed stage, they have lost their aroma and will not be suitable for potpourris or sachets, but they may be used in floral arrangements.

Remove all unwanted plant material (stems, leaves, etc.) and place on the dehydrator trays. Flowers can be dried with or without their stems. Plants shrink at least one-half of their original size and weight, and stems shrivel when dried. Dry flowers until crisp for use in dry potpourris and sachets, but only partially dry flowers for moist potpourris. After you have dated and labeled the dried flowers, store them in an airtight container in a dark place as excess of light quickly fades flowers.

Flower arrangements can be made with dried flowers, but wires must be used in place of stems. In addition to potpourris and sachets described below, dried flowers may also be used in cooking (added to jams and jellies) and in bathwater.

Potpourris

Potpourris are blends of flowers, herbs, spices, and a fixative. There are two types of potpourris: dry and moist. Dry potpourris last for one to two years; whereas moist potpourris last indefinitely, especially if moistened yearly with a little brandy. The dry potpourri, which is more attractive than the moist one, is used to fill decorative jars.

A fixative is added to potpourris to hold the fragrances for long periods of time. Orrisroot, the most commonly used fixative, has a violet scent. Calamus, musk, benzoin, storax, and ambergis are other fixatives that can be used. Most fixatives are available at drug stores, herb shops, or perfumery supply houses.

Dried roses are the most popular flower and usually the main scent in potpourris, but lilacs and violets also make lovely additions. Use whole dried flower petals, heads, leaves, and buds.

Lavender blossoms and mint blenders are herbs which are commonly used in potpourris; but almost any herb can be added, including rosemary, sweet marjoram, sage, basil, bay leaf, and oregano. When combining fragrances, be careful that one scent does not overpower the main one. Cinnamon stick or ground cinnamon, nutmeg, whole or ground cloves, and anise are common spices used in potpourris. Dried orange, lemon, tangerine, and grapefruit peel are other blenders that can be added to enhance the scent.

Herb Potpourri

1/2 cup dried lemon balm
1/2 cup dried spearmint
1/4 cup dried thyme
1 cup dried rosemary
1/2 cup dried sage
1/2 cup dried summer savory
12 cardamon seeds, crushed
1/4 cup dried lemon peel
2 tablespoons orrisroot
5 drops pure lemon extract
5 drops pure orange extract

Combine all ingredients in a crock and mix periodically. Put in an airtight container or a decorative jar.

Dry Potpourri

1 quart dried flowers
1 tablespoon fixative
1 tablespoon ground spices
2 tablespoons dried peels, leaves, or small pieces of fragrant wood
1 teaspoon sugar
1 teaspoon salt

In a large bowl thoroughly mix all ingredients. Cover and allow to sit for 4 to 6 weeks, stirring gently every other day. When potpourri begins to lose its smell, add a few drops of a scented oil to reactivate.

Moist Potpourri

1 quart partially dried flowers
1 quart partially dried herbs
1/4 cup dried peels, leaves, or small pieces of fragrant wood
2 tablespoons fixative
1/2 cup salt
3 tablespoons brown sugar
1/4 cup ground spices
2 tablespoons brandy

In a small bowl mix flowers, herbs, peels, and fixative. Combine salt, sugar, and spices. In a large bowl alternately layer dried ingredients and salt mixture, sprinkling a little of the brandy on each layer. Gently stir the mixture. Place mixture in an airtight container and stir every few days.

Sachets

Sachets are basically the same as dry potpourris; however, sachets are placed in material bags. (Homemade sachets, make great gift items.) Place sachets in drawers or closets to subtly perfume clothing. Sachets can also be placed in containers to perfume a room.

Sachets are also made with dried flowers, dried herbs, and spices. As in potpourris, roses are usually the main ingredient. Herbs, such as scented geraniums, rosemary, thyme, violets, and mints, are also added to sachets. Dried orange, lemon, lime, and grapefruit peel are often included to give sachets added fragrance.

To make a sachet, mix roses and your choice of other flowers, herbs, spices, and citrus peel in a large bowl. The mixture can be sprinkled with a little brandy to add to the already-rich fragrance. Stuff into material bags and sew closed.

BASIL

SWEET OR RED

GENERAL INFORMATION

Selection of fresh product for drying:
Cut green or red basil leaves about 6 weeks after planting. It is best to cut the leaves before the flowers open, but continued cutting can be made throughout the growing season.

Preparation for drying:
Dust leaves with a damp cloth or wash with cold water (wet leaves may turn dark brown when dried). Remove stem. Dry the leaf whole. Crush leaves just before using.

Characteristics of dried product:
Brittle.

Ways to use:
Add to any recipe containing tomatoes.

Make basil jelly and serve with crackers.

Make basil tea which has a clovelike flavor.

Use red and/or green leaves to make basil vinegar.

Mix with cream cheese and use to stuff celery.

Use to enhance the flavor of eggplant, zucchini, salads, meats, and eggs.

Use to scent bathwater.

RECIPE AND USE SUGGESTIONS

Pesto
1/2 cup olive oil
3 cloves garlic
1/3 cup dried basil
1/4 cup pine nuts or sunflower seeds
1 cup fresh parsley or spinach
1/2 cup Parmesan cheese

In a blender combine olive oil, garlic, and dried basil. Blend at high speed. Let stand 15 minutes. Gradually add pine nuts or sunflower seeds. Blend. Add fresh parsley or spinach (remove any coarse stems). Blend. Add grated Parmesan cheese. (Serve over spinach noodles, or use as a sandwich spread.)

Basil Bath
2 tablespoons dried basil leaves
1 small cotton bag

Place basil leaves in a small cotton bag. Tie bag over bathtub spout so that water filters through the bag, or add bag directly to bathwater. One bag can be used three times.

Basil Butter
1/2 cup butter or margarine, softened
2 tablespoons crushed dried basil
1 tablespoon crushed dried parsley
1 tablespoon lemon juice
1/4 cup grated Parmesan cheese

Combine ingredients in a small bowl. Mix well. Cover and refrigerate. (Serve over broiled tomatoes, steaks, or hamburgers.)

BAY LEAF

GENERAL INFORMATION

Selection of fresh product for drying:
Bay leaves can be picked throughout the year. Choose shiny, green, young leaves from this evergreen tree.

Preparation for drying:
Dust off whole leaves. Remove stem and any damaged or imperfect areas.

Characteristics of dried product:
Brittle.

Ways to use:
Use in tomato dishes and as a complement to meat.

Use to flavor fish chowders, tomato dishes, foul, custards, soups, and stews.

Use as a central ingredient in sachets, potpourris, and bouquet garnis.

Bay Leaf Potatoes

3-4 whole potatoes, peeled
Water
1 tablespoon dried onion
3 dried bay leaves
Butter or margarine
Salt and pepper

Place potatoes in a medium-sized saucepan and cover with water. Bring to a boil. Add onions and bay leaves. Cook until soft. Drain off liquid and remove bay leaves. Add butter or margarine and salt and pepper to taste.

Bay Leaf Bath

2 tablespoons crushed dried bay leaves
1/3 cup oatmeal
3-4 2-inch cotton bags

Combine crushed bay leaves and oatmeal. Place mixture in cotton bags. Attach bag over bathtub spout so that bathwater filters through the bag, or add directly to bathwater. Bags can be dried and reused.

CAMOMILE

GENERAL INFORMATION

Selection of fresh food for drying:
When the yellow-white daisylike flower buds form, harvest both the feathery leaf and the flowers. Camomile has an applelike fragrance and flavor.

Preparation for drying:
Dust off plant. Remove any brown or imperfect areas. Separate blossoms from leaves. Store flower head and leaves separately.

Characteristics of dried product:
Brittle.

Ways to use:
Use to make a delicious, soothing tea.

Make herb butter and serve on baked potatoes.

Use camomile as you would bay leaf.

Use to make wine.

Add camomile blossoms to sour cream.

Camomile White Sauce

2 tablespoons butter or margarine
2 tablespoons flour
1/2 cup milk
1/2 teaspoon salt
1/4 teaspoon pepper
1/8 teaspoon nutmeg
1 tablespoon crushed dried camomile

Melt butter or margarine in a small saucepan. Blend in flour. Cook 2 to 3 minutes. Add milk, salt, pepper, and nutmeg. Add camomile and cook until mixture thickens.

Herb Iced Tea

4 cups boiling water
3 teaspoons dried camomile
6 sprigs dried peppermint
6 sprigs lemon balm

Pour water over dried herbs and steep 15 minutes. Strain. Chill, and serve with ice cubes.

Camomile Tea

Dried camomile flower heads and leaves
Boiling water
Dried mint

Steep camomile in boiling water for 3 to 5 minutes. Strain. Serve with a sprig of dried mint.

Camomile-Apple Tea (Pictured on page 108)

Dried camomile
Boiling water
Dried apple pieces or peel
Honey
Dried orange peel

Prepare tea by steeping camomile in boiling water for 3 to 5 minutes. Strain. Add dried apple pieces or peel. Serve with honey and a piece of dried orange peel.

CHIVES

GENERAL INFORMATION

Selection of fresh product for drying:
Chives are one of the earliest plants to appear in the spring. Both leaves and bulbs can be dried. Clip the plant early and often to avoid the development of purple seed blossoms. The slender, bright green leaves can be harvested throughout the growing season. It is best to harvest chives before they flower. (After they flower, the flower-heads must be removed before drying.) To harvest bulb, dig it up, remove the dirt, wash, and halve.

Preparation for drying:
Snip the leaves at least 1 inch from the ground, then cut into desired lengths. Wash the bulbs and dry whole.

Characteristics of dried product:
Brittle.

Ways to use:
Sprinkle dried chives on salads and main dishes.

Use as a flavoring substitute for salt.

Add to omelets, soups, sauces, and cottage cheese.

Make chive vinegar and use in salad dressings.

RECIPE SUGGESTIONS

Chicken and Sour Cream with Chives
1 pint sour cream or yogurt
2 tablespoons dried chives
1 teaspoon dried tarragon
1/2 teaspoon salt
2 tablespoons vinegar
2 teaspoons sugar
1 tablespoon melted butter or margarine
1 2½-3 pound chicken, cut up
Salt
1/3 cup flour
Paprika

Combine sour cream or yogurt, dried chives, dried tarragon, 1/2 teaspoon salt, vinegar, and sugar in a medium-sized bowl. Stir until blended. Pour melted butter or margarine in a large baking dish. Sprinkle chicken with salt, coat with flour, then dip in sour cream mixture. Arrange in baking dish. Do not overlap. Sprinkle with paprika. Bake in a 400° F. oven for 45 minutes or until tender. Thoroughly mix any remaining sour cream mixture with pan drippings and spoon over chicken before serving. Serves 4 to 6.

Chives and Cream Cheese Filling
8 ounces cream cheese, softened
1 teaspoon finely chopped dried chives

In a small bowl mix cream cheese and chives. Keep refrigerated. (Use to fill celery stalks or spread on crackers.)

DANDELION

GENERAL INFORMATION

Selection of fresh product for drying:
Pick leaves before they reach maturity to avoid the bitter taste. Dandelion roots from two-year-old plants can be dug up and dried in the fall. Collect dandelion blossoms after the dew has evaporated and when the flowers are perfect.

Preparation for drying:
Dust off leaves and remove stem pieces. Pick flowers and remove stem. Dig roots and wash carefully. Split roots in half to dry.

Characteristics of dried product:
Brittle.

Ways to use:
Use in salads.

Make dandelion wine.

Use dandelion blossoms in teas and sachets.

RECIPE SUGGESTIONS

Female Tea
4 cups boiling water
2 tablespoons dried raspberry leaves
2 tablespoons dried dandelion flowers
1/2 teaspoon ground ginger
2 cups apple juice or cider
Honey

Pour boiling water over raspberry leaves, dandelion flowers, and ginger. Add apple juice or cider. Steep for 10 minutes. Strain. Add honey to taste. Makes 6 cups of tea.

Dandelion Root Tea
6 cups boiling water
1/3 cup dried dandelion root
Milk (optional)
Sugar or honey (optional)
Carob or cinnamon (optional)

Pour boiling water over dried dandelion root. Steep 10 minutes. Strain. If desired, add milk, sugar or honey, carob or cinnamon.

Camomile-Apple Tea (page 107) and dried orange slices with dainty Yam Tarts (page 51), Pear Bread (page 82), and Fig-Filled Cookies (page 77)

DILL

GENERAL INFORMATION

Selection of fresh product for drying:
Dill leaves and seeds can be dried. The yellow-green plumelike leaves which appear just as the flat-topped flowers open are best. Seeds have a stronger flavor than leaves. Dill seeds are collected from the flower heads.

Preparation for drying:
Dill leaves and seeds can be dried and stored on the stem. Seeds can be released by rubbing the flowers between your hands.

Characteristics of dried product:
Brittle.

Ways to use:
Use with sauerkraut, beans, beets, broccoli, and cauliflower.

Add to deviled eggs, cottage cheese, and cream cheese.

Make dill vinegar.

Make dill herb butter.

Use with fresh cucumbers.

Add to soups, stews, tomato juice, salads, and pickles.

RECIPE SUGGESTIONS

Dill Dip

8 ounces yogurt or sour cream

1 teaspoon Tabasco sauce

1 teaspoon dried dill

1/2 teaspoon dried onion or garlic powder

Place yogurt or sour cream in a small bowl. Add Tabasco sauce, dried dill, and dried onion or garlic powder. Mix. Keep refrigerated. (Serve with fresh vegetables, dried vegetable slices, potato or corn chips.)

Dill Deviled Eggs (Pictured on page 44)

6 eggs

1 teaspoon crushed dried dill

2 tablespoons mayonnaise

2 tablespoons cider vinegar

1/2 teaspoon salt

1/4 teaspoon pepper

Boil eggs for 10 to 12 minutes. Cool. Remove shells and cut eggs in half lengthwise. Remove yolks and mash until fine. Add the dried dill, mayonnaise, vinegar, salt, and pepper. Blend well. Fill whites with yolk mixture. Chill before serving. (Mixture can also be used in egg-salad sandwiches.) Makes 12.

GARLIC

GENERAL INFORMATION

Selection of fresh product for drying:
Garlic is a flat-leafed onion. The bulbs break into small sections called cloves, and each clove has a thin paperlike skin. Dig mature bulbs when the tops droop.

Preparation for drying:
Break bulbs into cloves and remove the paperlike skin. Dry cloves individually.

Characteristics of dried product:
Brittle.

Ways to use:
Make garlic vinegar.

Pulverize dried garlic to make garlic powder.

Make garlic butter and add dried parsley.

RECIPE SUGGESTIONS

Garlic Salt

2 parts salt

1 part powdered dried garlic

Mix ingredients. Use as a salt substitute or for seasoning.

Garlic-Curry Dip

1 teaspoon powdered dried garlic

1 teaspoon curry powder

1 tablespoon sugar

1 teaspoon powdered dried onion

1 teaspoon grated horseradish or 1/2 teaspoon dry horseradish

1 teaspoon cider vinegar

1/2 cup sour cream

1/2 cup mayonnaise

Combine garlic powder, curry powder, sugar, onion powder, horseradish, and cider vinegar. Add sour cream and mayonnaise, and mix well. Chill before serving. (Serve with chips, fresh vegetables, or dried vegetable chips.)

HORSERADISH

GENERAL INFORMATION

Selection of fresh product for drying:
Horseradish, also known as wild radish, is a perennial with large leaves, green to yellow-green in coloring. Dig this pungent root in the spring before the leaves appear on the plant, or wait until the end of the growing season.

Preparation for drying:
Wash root carefully. Cut off top and end. Peel. Slice into ¼-inch pieces.

Characteristics of dried product:
Hard.

Ways to use:
Pulverize hard pieces to make horseradish powder.

Add powder to coleslaw and salad dressings.

Use to make vinegar.

Add to mustard for horseradish mustard.

Make into a sauce to use with fish or meats.

RECIPE SUGGESTION

Horseradish Sauce
1/2 cup sour cream or yogurt
1/2 cup mayonnaise
1/4 cup grated fresh onion
1/2 teaspoon sugar
1/2 teaspoon powdered dried horseradish

Mix all ingredients. Chill before serving. (Use as a fancy mayonnaise, a dip for fondue, or add to egg salad.)

LAVENDER

GENERAL INFORMATION

Selection of fresh product for drying:
The small lavender flowers are borne on long-stemmed, slender spikes. Available in two common varieties, English and French, the beautiful purple flowers bloom on a grey-green stem.

Preparation for drying:
Cut flower spikes when the first flowers begin to open. The entire plant can be dried. Dust to clean. Separate leaves from stems after drying. Lavender holds its scent beautifully after drying.

Characteristics of dried product:
Crushable.

Ways to use:
Make lavender sugar to sweeten pancakes and desserts.

Garnish salads, fruit punches, and frostings.

Make a tea from lavender blossoms (add dried mint and rosemary leaves).

Make lavender vinegar from blossoms.

Add to the bathwater.

Add dried herbs to water. Filter and use for a skin freshener.

RECIPE AND USE SUGGESTIONS

Lavender Sachet (Pictured on page 116)
1/2 cup dried lavender leaves and flowers
1/2 cup dried orange peel pieces
Small cloth bags

Combine lavender and orange peel. Fill cloth bags and stitch closed. Place in drawers and closets to freshen and scent clothes. Lavender sachet can also be used to scent bathwater.

Lavender Jelly
Dried lavender blossoms
Hot apple jelly (recipe below)

Place 1 tablespoon of lavender blossoms in the bottom of each small, sterile jelly jar. Pour in hot apple jelly and seal. (Serve with lamb and other meats.)

Apple Jelly
Tart cooking apples
Water
Sugar

Wash and core apples. Cut into eighths. Discard any blemished areas. Place in a large pot and add just enough water to cover apples. Cook over medium heat until apples are very soft. Pour apples and water through a jelly bag or several layers of cheesecloth, bringing corners of cloth together. Gently squeeze bag to extract all the juice. Measure juice. Bring to a vigorous boil. Skim off foam and add 3/4 cup sugar for each cup of boiling juice. Boil rapidly to jelly stage, approximately 20 minutes. Pour into sterile jars and seal.

LILAC

GENERAL INFORMATION

Selection of fresh product for drying:
Select completely opened flowers just after the night dew has evaporated.

Preparation for drying:
Leave flowerets on the smallest stem. Place on trays; try not to have flowers overlapping. Dehydrate for 1 hour. If flowers are not dry, return to dehydrator and continue drying. When dry, pinch the stems and rub off the flowers.

Characteristics of dried product:
Crisp.

Ways to use:
Add to sachets and potpourris.

Use dry flowers to decorate cakes and cookies.

Use in flower arrangements.

USE SUGGESTION

Lilac Potpourri (Pictured on page 116)
2/3 cup dried lilacs
1/3 cup dried cloves
2 tablespoons dried lavender
2 tablespoons dried spearmint
4 tablespoons dried rosemary
4 tablespoons dried lemon mint or lemon verbena
2 tablespoons orrisroot
4 drops lavender oil

Mix all ingredients and place in an airtight glass container.

MINT

CATNIP

GENERAL INFORMATION

Selection of fresh product for drying:
The heart-shaped, gray-green leaves of catnip are deeply indented on the sides. The stems are square. Do not pick yellow leaves.

Preparation for drying:
Dust leaves (leaves that have been washed turn dark). Remove leaves from stem, and dry leaves whole.

Characteristics of dried product:
Brittle.

Ways to use:
Make a refreshing tea (add other mints, honey, and lemon).

Add to sachets and potpourris.

Make scented pillows.

USE SUGGESTION

Catnip Toy
Firm double-knit fabric or tightly woven cotton
Yarn
Felt (color should contrast with body color)
Cotton balls
1 tablespoon dried catnip
Embroidery floss

Cut out one base. Fold fabric with right sides together and cut out two bodies. Cut two ears from felt. Braid yarn and knot the end to form a 2½-inch tail. Place two body sections right sides together and sew a ¼-inch top seam from A to B. Clip curves. Pin tail to base at point B, extending tail inward. Pin right side of body to right side of base, matching points A and B on base and body pieces. Sew from the middle of one side to nose. Leave needle in fabric and pivot to form point. Continue sewing around body and past tail. Leave a 1½-inch opening. Trim seam (especially at nose). Turn mouse right side out. Using a needle, gently pull the nose all the way out. Stuff two cotton balls in the nose and head. Add catnip. Continue stuffing with cotton until firm. Hand sew opening together. Fold base of ears together and hand sew to each side of head. With embroidery floss make eyes (French knots), nose (a few straight stitches), and whiskers (knot threat 1-inch from end, run needle through nose, knot other side, and clip 1-inch from knot). Use as a toy for cats.

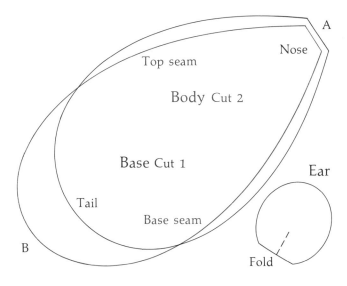

A

Nose

Top seam

Body Cut 2

Base Cut 1

Ear

Tail

Base seam

B

Fold

PEPPERMINT AND SPEARMINT

GENERAL INFORMATION

Selection of fresh product for drying:
There are many varieties of mint. All varieties have a square stem and pinnate leaves. Pick leaves just as flowering begins.

Preparations for drying:
Remove leaves from stem. Dry leaves whole. Leaves darken in color when dried.

Characteristics of dried product:
Brittle.

Ways to use:
Add to fruit salads, cream cheese, and lamb stew.

Make mint jelly.

Add to honey or sugar.

Make mint vinegar. (Use very strong mint vinegar for insect repellent.)

Use to make sauces to serve with meat.

Add to cooking vegetables.

Make mint herb butter.

Make mint mustard.

Make mint cushions for use as air fresheners.

Add to sachets, potpourris, and baths.

RECIPE SUGGESTIONS

Candy Mint
An alternative drying procedure.

Fresh mint sprigs

Water

Powdered sugar

Dip fresh mint sprigs in water. Shake off excess water and coat with powdered sugar. Dry and use as a garnish.

Apple-Mint Tea (Pictured on page 76)

1 part dried apple peels
1 part dried mint leaves
Small dried apple pieces
Boiling water
Nutmeg
Cinnamon
Honey

Pulverize dried apple peels. Add dried mint leaves and dried apple pieces. Pour boiling water over ingredients and steep 5 minutes. Strain. Add nutmeg, cinnamon, and honey to taste.

Chocolate Chip Mint Cookies

1 cup firmly packed brown sugar
1/2 cup white sugar
1 cup butter or margarine, softened
1 teaspoon vanilla
2 eggs
2 cups flour
1/3 cup crushed dried mint
1½ teaspoons baking soda
1/2 teaspoon salt
2 cups chocolate chips or carob chips

Combine brown sugar, white sugar, butter or margarine, and vanilla in a large bowl. Mix well. Add eggs and blend until creamy. In a separate bowl mix flour, mint, baking soda, and salt. Add dry ingredients to creamed mixture. Mix. Add chocolate chips or carob chips, and stir gently. Drop by teaspoonfuls onto ungreased cookie sheets. Bake in a 375° F. oven for 10 to 12 minutes or until done. Makes 6 dozen.

Carrots in Mint Butter
Used by permission of *Herb Forum.*

2 cups sliced dried carrots
2 cups salted water
2 tablespoons butter or margarine
1 teaspoon sugar
2 tablespoons crushed dried mint

In a medium-sized saucepan soak carrots in salted water for 1 hour, then cook until barely tender. Drain off water. Saute carrots slowly in butter or margarine and sugar. Add dried mint before serving. Serves 6.

NASTURTIUM

GENERAL INFORMATION

Selection of fresh product for drying:
The flowers, leaves, and seedpods are edible and therefore suitable for drying. Harvest almost anytime. Pick seedpods when mature, yet green. Pick flowers when fully opened. The round, saucerlike leaves have a spicy, pungent flavor. Nasturtium petals have a peppery taste.

Preparation for drying:
Dust, or wash if necessary. To dry the flowers, remove from the stems. Flowers shrivel and darken in color when dried.

Characteristics of dried product:
Brittle.

Ways to use:
Crush and use with cream cheese for spreads.

Use blossoms, leaves, and seeds in green salads.

Add to sauces and omelets.

Sprinkle over cold soups.

Make nasturtium vinegar from leaves and blossoms.

Use nasturtium seeds in place of capers.

Add nasturtium seeds to teas.

Use in iced drinks.

Substitute for watercress or lettuce.

RECIPE SUGGESTION

Nasturtium-Cucumber Salad
  2 tablespoons wine or tarragon vinegar
  3/4 teaspoon dry mustard
  6 tablespoons olive oil
  1/4 teaspoon salt
  1 tablespoon dried tarragon
  1/2 cup small dried nasturtium leaf pieces
  2 fresh cucumbers, peeled and sliced
  Lettuce
  Dried nasturtium flowers

In a bowl mix wine or tarragon vinegar, dry mustard, olive oil, salt, and tarragon. Add nasturtium leaves and cucumbers. Marinate at least 30 minutes before draining and serving on lettuce leaves. Garnish with dried nasturtium flowers. Serves 2 to 4.

OREGANO

GENERAL INFORMATION

Selection of fresh product for drying:
Oregano, also known as wild marjoram, has a stronger flavor, slightly larger leaves, and is a hardier plant than sweet marjoram. It has a thymelike scent and flavor. Harvest oregano just as the white flowers appear. Oregano is an important herb in Italian and Spanish dishes and an essential ingredient in chili powder.

Preparation for drying:
Dust to clean. Remove leaves from stem. Store whole after dried. Crush just before using.

Characteristics of dried product:
Brittle.

Ways to use:
Add to tomato dishes, especially tomato juice.

Make oregano herb butter and use over vegetables.

Use with pizza, spaghetti, meats, salads, sauces, eggs, and fish.

Make oregano vinegar.

Add to salads and salad dressings.

RECIPE SUGGESTION

Oregano Salad Dressing
Used by permission of *Herb Forum*.
  1/2 cup olive oil
  1/4 cup lemon juice
  1 teaspoon salt
  1/2 teaspoon pepper
  1 clove garlic, minced
  1 teaspoon dried oregano
  1/8 teaspoon sugar

Mix all ingredients in a blender or shake in a jar. (Serve over tossed green salad.) Makes 3/4 cup.

PARSLEY

GENERAL INFORMATION

Selection of fresh product for drying:
Curly-leaf and flat-leaf varieties can be dried. Harvest parsley before it flowers. Parsley root can also be dried.

Preparation for drying:
Cut parsley branches from stem. Shake or wash to clean. Inspect parsley and remove any brown areas. When dry, separate clusters from the stem. Store clusters. Wash and dry root whole.

Characteristics of dried product:
Brittle.

Ways to use:
Combine with melted butter or margarine and serve with vegetables.

Make parsley tea from parsley root.

Add parsley to soups, stews, and sauces just before serving.

Garnish chicken, fish, creamy and French-type salad dressings, and chip dips.

Use tea as a hair rinse.

RECIPE SUGGESTIONS

Parsley Salt
1 part dried parsley
1 part salt

Pulverize parsley and add salt. Store in an airtight glass jar. (Use as a salt substitute.)

Parsley Butter
1 tablespoon pulverized dried parsley
1/4 pound butter or margarine, melted
1/2 teaspoon paprika

Blend parsley, melted butter or margarine, and paprika. Keep refrigerated. (Use to season vegetables, or spread on French bread and warm in oven.)

Parsley Potatoes
6-8 medium-sized potatoes
1 tablespoon butter or margarine
1 small onion, grated
1 tablespoon dried parsley
1/2 teaspoon salt
1/4 teaspoon pepper

In saucepan boil potatoes with skins until tender. Drain off water. Peel. Add butter or margarine, onion, parsley, salt, and pepper. Serve hot.

Parsley Tea
4 cups water
1/3 cup dried parsley
Fresh lemon slice (optional)

Boil water. Pour over dried parsley or a tea ball full of dried parsley. Steep 3 to 5 minutes. Strain. Add lemon slice if desired.

ROSE

HIPS AND PETALS

GENERAL INFORMATION

Selection of fresh product for drying:
Harvest rose petals when the weather is hot and dry and the petals have just reached full bloom. The seedpods of the roses, known as rose hips, are the natural fruit of the rose bush. These small, berrylike pods form as the petals fall off. Harvest when bright red.

Preparation for drying:
Remove ends and stems before drying blossoms. Cut off the white heels/claws from the rose hips, cut seedpods in half, and remove seeds before drying. For use as a garnish, dip petals in egg whites and powdered sugar, and dry. The rose remains fragrant after drying.

Characteristics of dried product:
Brittle.

Ways to use:
Make rose-petal or rose-hip jelly.

Use to make teas—hot or iced.

Add petals to desserts for a delicate flavor.

Make rose vinegar.

Use petals to make rose sugar or honey.

Make rose butter.

Add rose hips to soups, sauces, poultry stuffings, and desserts.

Add petals to sachets and potpourris.

RECIPE AND USE SUGGESTIONS

Rose Hip Tea
1 teaspoon crushed dried rose hips
1 cup boiling water
Honey
Lemon

Place rose hips in boiling water. Steep 10 to 12 minutes. Strain. Add honey and lemon to taste.

Rose Hip Jello Salad

1/4 cup dried rose hips
1-2 cups water
1 3-ounce package lemon or orange gelatin
1 cup hot water
1/4 cup chopped walnuts
Lettuce

In a small saucepan cook dried rose hips in water until tender. Puree in blender. Measure puree and add enough cold water to make 1 cup of puree. Place lemon or orange gelatin in a bowl and add 1 cup hot water. Stir until gelatin is dissolved. Add rose hip puree and chopped walnuts. Refrigerate until gelatin sets. Serve on a bed of lettuce. Serves 4.

Rose Potpourri

3/4 cup dried rose petals
1/4 cup dried mint leaves
2 tablespoons dried lavender flowers
2 tablespoons powdered dried orange peel
1 tablespoon dried bay leaf pieces
1 tablespoon dried stick cinnamon pieces
1 tablespoon orrisroot
3 drops lavender oil

Combine all ingredients. Stir. Place in a decorative airtight jar.

Rose Water

1 cup dried rose petals
1 quart cold water

Place rose petals and water in a pan. Let sit 1 hour. Bring almost to a boil, cool, and strain. (Use for washing and bathing.)

ROSE GERANIUM

GENERAL INFORMATION

Selection of fresh product for drying:
There are many scents of geraniums: rose, lemon, mint, orange, apple, etc. All can be dried. Cut leaves from mature plants anytime. The rose geranium has a spicy rose smell.

Preparation for drying:
Dust leaves and remove from stem. Dry and store whole leaves.

Characteristics of dried product:
Brittle.

Ways to use:
Use to flavor fruit.

Use to garnish salads, cakes, and meats.

Use to flavor desserts, jellies, or gelatins.

Make rose geranium vinegar.

Make rose geranium jelly or jam, or add a leaf to apple jelly.

Add a leaf as accent to peaches and pears.

Mix with mint for a spicy tea (add dried orange peel and a few cloves).

Crumble a few leaves to perfume a room.

Use with lavender mixes.

Use to scent bathwater.

Add to potpourris and sachets.

RECIPE SUGGESTION

Rose Geranium Sweet Rolls

1 cup milk
1/2 pound butter or margarine
2 teaspoons salt
1½ cups sugar
2 tablespoons dry yeast
1 cup warm water
2 eggs, beaten
6-6½ cups flour

FILLING:

1 cup butter or margarine
1/2 cup small dried rose geranium leaf pieces
1 cup sugar or honey
1 tablespoon powdered dried orange peel

In a small saucepan scald milk. Combine butter or margarine, salt, and sugar in a large mixing bowl. Pour scalded milk over butter mixture. Set aside to cool. Soften yeast in water. Let yeast become active (about 5 to 10 minutes), then stir down. Add yeast to lukewarm butter mixture. Add eggs to mixture. Stir. Add 3 cups flour, and mix well. Gradually stir in 3 to 3½ cups more flour until dough pulls away from the sides of the bowl. Cover and refrigerate dough overnight. Dough will keep a week in the refrigerator after it has been punched down two or three times the first day and once each following day. Remove dough several hours before using. To prepare filling, melt butter or margarine. Add rose geranium leaves, sugar or honey, and powdered orange peel. Roll dough into a large rectangle, approximately ¼-inch thick. Spread filling evenly to the edges. Roll as for jelly roll. Cut into 1-inch pieces. Place cut-side down in greased muffin cups. Let rise 1/2 hour or until double in size. Bake in a 400° F. oven for 20 minutes. Makes 2 dozen.

A potpourri of potpourris (from left to right): Lavender Sachet (page 111), Rose Potpourri, Lilac Potpourri (page 112), and dried lavender.

ROSEMARY

GENERAL INFORMATION

Selection of fresh product for drying:
The grey-green needlelike leaves of rosemary are rather leathery and have a spicy pine scent. Remove leaves before the plant blossoms. The pale blue orchidlike flowers can also be dried.

Preparation for drying:
Dry the stems and the needlelike leaves. Remove the leaves from the stem before storing.

Characteristics of dried product:
Brittle.

Ways to use:
Make rosemary vinegar.

Infuse honey with dried blossoms.

Use to flavor meats.

Use to season vegetables.

Sprinkle over the hot coals when barbecuing.

Use to scent baths and to rinse hair.

Add to sachets and potpourris.

RECIPE AND USE SUGGESTIONS

Rosemary Jelly
Dried rosemary blossoms
Hot apple jelly (page 111)

Place 1 tablespoon of rosemary blossoms in the bottom of each small, sterile jar. Pour in hot apple jelly and seal. (Serve with lamb, pork, poultry, or veal.)

Rosemary Tea
1 teaspoon dried rosemary
1 cup boiling water
Lemon juice
Honey

Steep rosemary in boiling water for 3 to 5 minutes. Strain. Add lemon juice and honey to taste.

Dried Rosemary Sachet
Dried rosemary
Dried lavender
Dried lemon peel
Cotton bags

Blend rosemary, lavender, and dried lemon peel. Stuff inside bags and sew closed. (Use to perfume lingerie or other clothing.)

Rosemary Sugar
1 part dried rosemary
5 parts sugar

Combine rosemary and sugar. Store in an airtight container for at least 1 week before using. Shake every day. (Use in pancakes, desserts, and other dishes.)

Rosemary Butter
Used by permission of *Herb Forum.*

1/2 cup butter or margarine
1 teaspoon crushed dried rosemary

Melt butter or margarine in a small saucepan. Add rosemary. (Use as a basting sauce for barbecued fish or chicken.)

SAGE

GENERAL INFORMATION

Selection of fresh product for drying:
All varieties of sage can be dried. Begin harvesting the grey-green oblong leaves early in the season. Sage can be harvested before and after the plant blooms.

Preparation for drying:
Shake or dust plant to clean leaves. Remove stems and any dry leaves.

Characteristics of dried product:
Brittle.

Ways to use:

Use for stuffings.

Add to cheeses.

Make sage tea (flavor with lemon and honey).

Make sage butter.

Make sage jelly and serve with poultry and pork.

Add to biscuits and serve with meat.

Bake with squash.

Use to season vegetables.

Make sage vinegar.

Sprinkle in eggs.

Add to potpourris and sachets.

Use to scent bathwater and to rinse hair.

RECIPE AND USE SUGGESTIONS

Sage Cheese

8 ounces cream cheese, softened
1 tablespoon minced green onion
1/2 teaspoon crushed dried sage
Poppy seeds or chopped nuts

Combine cream cheese, green onion, and sage. Mold into a ball and roll in poppy seeds or chopped nuts. Refrigerate to blend flavors. Bring to room temperature before serving. (Serve with crackers.)

Sage Bath

Dried sage leaves
Cotton bag

Place dried sage leaves in a small cotton bag. Tie bag over the bathtub spout and let bathwater filter through the leaves.

SWEET MARJORAM

GENERAL INFORMATION

Selection of fresh product for drying:
Pick small, oval, gray-green leaves before plant blooms.

Preparation for drying:
Remove leaves from stem.

Characteristics of dried product:
Brittle.

Ways to use:
Make marjoram butter.

Add to salads, vegetables, fish, and sauces.

Make marjoram jelly and serve with pork chops, pork roast, or venison.

Add to orange marmalade.

Make marjoram vinegar which is especially good with meats.

RECIPE SUGGESTIONS

Sweet Marjoram Dressing
Used by permission of *Herb Forum*.

1/2 teaspoon dried sweet marjoram
1/2 cup olive oil
1/4 cup lemon juice
1 teaspoon salt
1/2 teaspoon pepper
1 clove garlic, minced
1/8 teaspoon sugar

Mix all ingredients in blender. Refrigerate to allow flavors to blend. (Serve on tossed green salad.)

Sweet Marjoram Tea

1 cup boiling water
1 teaspoon dried sweet marjoram
Dried mint

Pour hot water over sweet marjoram. Steep 5 minutes. Strain. Add dried mint to taste.

TARRAGON

GENERAL INFORMATION

Selection of fresh product for drying:
Harvest tarragon throughout the growing season. Process leaves before they turn yellow. These narrow, dark-green leaves have an aniselike flavor.

Preparation for drying:
Dust leaves to clean. Dry leaves on stems, then remove leaves and crush before storing.

Characteristics of dried product:
Crisp.

Ways to use:
Add to white sauce.

Add a small amount to tomato dishes, especially tomato juice.

Season vegetables, meats, seafood, salads, and eggs.

Make tarragon mustard.

RECIPE SUGGESTIONS

Tarragon-Grape Jelly

3 cups grape juice

2 teaspoons dried tarragon

2½ teaspoons lemon juice

1 1¾-ounce package powdered pectin

3½ cups sugar

In a large kettle combine the grape juice and tarragon. Heat to scalding. Remove from heat and let stand 15 minutes. Strain through cheesecloth. Return liquid to kettle, and add lemon juice and pectin. Cook over high heat, stirring constantly, until mixture comes to a full boil. Stir in sugar. Cook until mixture reaches a rolling boil. Boil exactly 1 minute, stirring constantly. Remove from heat, skim off foam, pour into ½-pint sterile jars, and seal. Makes 2 pints.

VARIATIONS
Both herb and juice can be changed to obtain different jellies. For example, try grapefruit and thyme, grapefruit and marjoram, apple and mint, cranberry juice and sage.

Tarragon Mayonnaise

1 teaspoon dried tarragon

1 cup mayonnaise

1/4 teaspoon pulverized dried celery

Blend tarragon, mayonnaise, and celery. Refrigerate in an airtight container. (Use as a salad dressing.)

THYME

GENERAL INFORMATION

Selection of fresh product for drying:
English, German, French, and Spanish are a few varieties available. The small leaves have a pungent, spicy scent. Dry the leaves and the flowering tops.

Preparation for drying:
Shake to clean. Dry leaves on the stem. After dehydration, separate leaves from stems.

Characteristics of dried product:
Brittle.

Ways to use:
Make thyme tea.

Add to tuna fish, poultry, chowders, stuffing, soups, and stews.

Make herb bread and herb butter.

Use to season dressings for salads.

Make thyme vinegar.

Make thyme jam and jelly.

Sprinkle on kitchen burner for a room freshener.

RECIPE SUGGESTION

Carrot-Thyme Pudding

4 fresh carrots

3 small scallions, chopped

3 tablespoons butter or margarine, melted

1/2 teaspoon salt

1/4 teaspoon pepper

1 teaspoon dried thyme

1/3 cup flour

4 eggs

2 cups chicken stock

Peel, slice, and cook carrots until tender. Puree carrots and scallions in blender. Add melted butter or margarine, salt, pepper, thyme, and flour. Add eggs, one at a time, blending well after each. Add stock and blend well. Pour into a lightly buttered 1-quart baking dish and place in a pan of water. Water should come well up the sides of the dish. Bake in a 325° F. oven for 60 minutes or until a knife inserted in the center comes out clean. Serves 4.

INDEX

Designed and illustrated by Steven M. Larsen. Photography by Longin Lonczyna. Typeset by Twin Typographers in Elegante and Elegante semi-bold. Color separations provided by Ridges Color Center. Printed by Sun Lithographing Company on 70 pound Mead B/W dull. Bound in Holliston Kevtone C matte by Hiller Industries. All of Salt Lake City, Utah.

Magic Aire II Food Dehydrator™

Nothing captures and preserves the fresh-picked flavor and nutrition of fruits, vegetables and meats like the Magic Aire II dehydrator. The secret lies in its design: hot, dry air passes around and through food, substantially reducing drying time, minimizing nutrient and flavor loss, and saving you energy.

The Magic Aire II's 10 stackable trays hold over ¼ bushel of produce in approximately 12 square feet of drying area. You can dry as much or as little as you wish—use up to ten individual trays or as few as two. Magic Aire II trays are durable, virtually immune to scars and stains, and made of an FDA approved material. The dehydrator weighs only 11½ pounds.

This innovative dehydrator has a 500 watt heater and is designed for continuous, safe 24-hour operation. The Magic Aire II is UL and CSA approved, and comes with a full two year warranty from the date of purchase.

GARDEN MAGIC SPROUTER TRAYS

Part of the 'magic' of the Magic Aire II is that its stackable dehydrator trays can also be used with the sprouting tray inserts. These inserts allow just the right amount of space between trays for air circulation and sprout growth. You simply stack the trays inside the Magic Aire II's drying trays and place them on your kitchen counter (not on the Magic Aire II base). Add a little water and let nature do the rest.

NEW AND IMPROVED FRUIT LEATHER SHEETS

Fruit and vegetable leathers are easily made with the accessory fruit leather sheets. Fruit leather is delicious and nutritious low-calorie fruit candy. Kids love it! Designed exclusively for use in the Magic Aire II dehydrator, these fruit leather sheets are made of an FDA approved material and will not warp, stain or break during use. The fruit leather sheets are also dishwasher safe and offer a no-spill edge. No Magic Aire II dehydrator is complete without these new and improved fruit leather sheets!

MESH TRAY INSERTS

These accessory items allow the efficient drying of smaller or diced fruits and vegetables, as well as the quick removal of the toughest dried-on foods. The inserts are also dishwasher safe and are made of an FDA approved material.

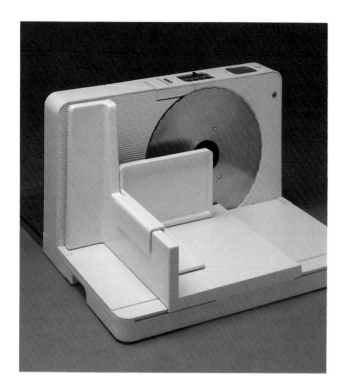

Bosch Electronic Slicer

The Bosch Electronic Slicer is an indispensable companion to the Magic Aire II dehydrator. Food that is sliced to a uniform thickness by this slicer dries more quickly and is more attractive in appearance. Slicing food for drying is made beautifully simple and amazingly fast with the Bosch Electronic Slicer.

But there's more you can do with this excellent slicer. You can prepare your own specialty cuts of meat—from deli-thin cuts of pastrami for sandwiches, to thick, juicy slices of prime rib. Homemade bread is effortlessly and evenly sliced. And, cheese can be sliced, wrapped and frozen until ready for use.

A handy speed adjustment on the Bosch Electronic Slicer automatically regulates the speed of the stainless steel blade. 'On' and 'Off' operation is controlled by a simple push-button release. This button may be depressed to operate the machine automatically, allowing you both hands free—a special Bosch safety feature. A workboard, separate serving tray, clamp, and two individual slice holders for large and small items are all standard features.

The Bosch Electronic Slicer features a one year warranty effective from the date of purchase.

Bosch Kitchen Machine

The Bosch Kitchen Machine is the ideal companion to the Magic Aire II Food Dehydrator. Here is the one appliance that is fully equipped to prepare foods for dehydrating as well as to assist in using dried foods to make delicious family favorites.

Standard equipment includes a blender for preparing fruit leathers and for pulverizing dried foods into flakes and powders. The standard mixing bowl, made of impact-resistant plastic, holds up to 8½ pounds of dough, and its splatter-free ring helps keep contents inside. The kneading arm is strong enough for heavy-duty kneading, while the wire whips provide delicate whipping.

Over twenty attachments enable the Bosch Kitchen Machine to perform nearly every food preparation function short of actual cooking. When preparing foods for drying, the Slicer and Shredder, Extrusion Shredder, and Berry Press are a great boon.

Famous Bosch engineering results in long, low-maintenance performance. The appliance carries a full one-year warranty from date of purchase.

Magic Mill III™ Flour Mill

Space-age technology is at your fingertips when you use the Magic Mill III to convert whole grains into flour. Through the revolutionary micro-milling™ process, grains are not milled but actually exploded into minute, uniform particles of flour.

The Magic Mill III unlocks the natural goodness, vital nutrition, and essential bran fiber in whole grains. It produces fresh whole flour for every-day kitchen use. In addition to wheat, the Magic Mill III mills rice, barley, rye, soybeans, and many other grains.

The Magic Mill III features automatic flour pan locks, easy texture selection, a 19 cup stainless steel flour pan, six cup grain hopper, safe, recessed operating dials and an easy-clean design. It's also incredibly fast; milling up to 1.8 pounds of flour per minute. This compact mill weighs only nine pounds and comes with a full two year warranty from the date of purchase.

The Golden Fitness Machine™

There are rebounders and there are rebounders, but there is only one Golden Fitness Machine. The Golden Fitness Machine is quite simply one of the finest—if not the finest—rebounders available.

Everything about this rebounder shouts of quality. The Golden Fitness Machine's three-ply, eight row mat stitching ensures added strength and durability.

And, rip-stop nylon backing is sewn to an attractive, scuff-proof vinyl protective cover. This prevents the springs from wearing holes through the foam and protective cover.

These are only two of the outstanding design features that Golden Fitness Machine owners enjoy daily. The Golden Fitness Machine, which comes with a full five year warranty, is yet another fine product in the Magic Mill tradition.

CLIP AND MAIL THIS COUPON FOR MORE INFORMATION.

Please send me more information on the following
Magic Mill and Bosch appliances:

☐ Magic Aire II Food Dehydrator
☐ Bosch Electronic Slicer
☐ Bosch Kitchen Machine
☐ Bosch II
☐ Magic Mill III Grain Mill
☐ Golden Fitness Machine

_____

_____

_____

_____

_____

Name _____

Address _____

City _____ State _____

Zip _____ Telephone _____

Mail to:

Magic Mill
235 West 200 South
Salt Lake City, Utah 84101

(801) 322-1668

To order DEHYDRATION MADE SIMPLE:

Please send me _____ copies of *Dehydration Made Simple* at $11.95 each plus $1.00 per book for shipping and handling. Enclosed is my check or money order for $ _____ . (Utah residents, please add 5 percent sales tax.)

Name _____

Address _____

City _____

State _____ Zip _____

Telephone _____

Please send me _____ copies of *Dehydration Made Simple* at $11.95 each plus $1.00 per book for shipping and handling. Enclosed is my check or money order for $ _____ . (Utah residents, please add 5 percent sales tax.)

Name _____

Address _____

City _____

State _____ Zip _____

Telephone _____

To give DEHYDRATION MADE SIMPLE:

Please send _____ copies of *Dehydration Made Simple* to the address(es) below. Enclosed is my check or money order for $11.95 per book plus $1.00 per book for shipping and handling. (Utah residents, please add 5 percent sales tax.)

Name _____

Address _____

City _____

State _____ Zip _____

Name _____

Address _____

City _____

State _____ Zip _____

Please send _____ copies of *Dehydration Made Simple* to the address(es) below. Enclosed is my check or money order for $11.95 per book plus $1.00 per book for shipping and handling. (Utah residents, please add 5 percent sales tax.)

Name _____

Address _____

City _____

State _____ Zip _____

Name _____

Address _____

City _____

State _____ Zip _____

☐ I would like more information on the Magic Aire II Food Dehydrator.

☐ I would like a free demonstration in my home of the Magic Mill and Bosch appliances.

☐ I would like to know how I can become a Magic Mill Dealer.

Mail to:

Magic Mill
235 West 200 South
Salt Lake City, Utah 84101

☐ I would like more information on the Magic Aire II Food Dehydrator.

☐ I would like a free demonstration in my home of the Magic Mill and Bosch appliances.

☐ I would like to know how I can become a Magic Mill Dealer.

Mail to:

Magic Mill
235 West 200 South
Salt Lake City, Utah 84101

☐ Please include with each book a gift card in my name with the following message:

_____

_____

_____

Sender's name _____

Mail to:

Magic Mill
235 West 200 South
Salt Lake City, Utah 84101

☐ Please include with each book a gift card in my name with the following message:

_____

_____

_____

Sender's name _____

Mail to:

Magic Mill
235 West 200 South
Salt Lake City, Utah 84101

Special Binder-Ready Version

- This loose-leaf alternative will save you money

- Offers a flexible format

- Nonrefundable if shrink-wrap is removed

SIXTH EDITION

MARKETING THE CORE

Kerin & Hartley

McGraw Hill Education